THE PAPERBACK FANATIC

FANATICAL THOUGHTS

As I type this in late August 2020, the UK is still emerging from the COVID-19 lockdown. It's been 154 days since the first official lockdown was issued by the government. The world seems a very different place and we're still not out of it. What better way to distract yourself than with 64 pages of Fanatical reporting on paperbacks about disasters, viruses, and plagues, as well as a study of authors who have experienced true lockdown by serving hard-time. Finished off with snappy and erudite reviews of an array of vintage paperbacks related to this issue's contents. Who knew the end of the world could be so fun?

In case that isn't a sufficient dose of apocalyptica for your tastes, than I have also published **Pulp Apocalypse**, with 100 pages devoted to post-bomb action, romance and mutants. Available through Amazon.

I was sad to see Grady **Paperbacks from Hell** Hendrix announcing on FB that Scott Gronmark had passed away from cancer. You may have known Scott through his horror pseudonym of Nick Sharman, authoring lurid titles such as **Childmare** and **Judgement Day**, but I also regarded him as one of the last survivors that worked in New English Library, the cult British publisher during their golden age, and an awful lot of paperback lore passed away with Scott.

Onto more positive news, a number of knowledgeable people have been popping upon You Tube with vintage paperback related videos to entertain you when you are "working from home". The legendary Gary Lovisi of **Paperback Parade** is proving to be more prolific than Jess Franco, with a truly eclectic range of paperback musings, and Jules Burt recently showcased a true motherlode of a vintage paperback acquisition as well as another lowdown on repairing books.

In the world of the podcast, Eric Compton and Tom Simon continue to deliver a consistently informative and entertaining weekly podcast in **The Paperback Warrior**, with Paul Bishop and Richard Prosch in hot pursuit with their **Six Gun Justice** podcast. I was interviewed for a recent **Six Gun** podcast about my passion for fanzine publishing, which was a blast. If you want to understand the type of mind behind 80+ fanzines over the last few decades, then tune in. I think the script-writers for the third season of **Mindhunter** will find all the material they need.

I am also delighted to have contributed to the third of the Stephen Jones edited **Art of Horror** series, with a chapter on paperbacks in the forthcoming **Art of Pulp Horror**. I imagine it will be published by the time you read this. It's a grown-up professional book where I had to use proper grammar and everythink.

I am already beavering away on the next set of publications which will take me well into 2021. They include a Crime Special of **The Sleazy Reader** which will include true-crime magazines, Harlan Ellison's crime short stories, sleazy fiction digests, Mafia paperbacks, pre-code crime comics and more. Then an all-military special of **Men of Violence**, with a mix of reviews and articles on war fiction across the eras. And then it will be a choice between a Panther Books special of **Pulp Horror** or an EC/DC comics special of **Monster Maniacs**. It's a "special" time here at Fanatic HQ!

New contributions always welcome, so please drop me a line if you are interested.

All the best.

Justin

thepaperbackfanatic@sky.com

Issue 44
Published August 2020

Edited by Justin Marriott
Copy-edited and proofread by Tom Tesarek

Special thanks to all of this issue's contributors and scanners.
Jim O'Brien, Scott Carlson, Steve Carroll, Sean Nodland, Darrin Venticinque

FANATICAL CONTENTS

GIL COHEN; ONE MAN ARMY

Return of the Mack!

A review of the new volume devoted to the iconic cover artist for Mack Bolan The Executioner.

Page 4

DISASTER 70!

Planes, trains and automobiles!

A look at disaster novels. Rather than disastrous novels. Don't worry the Star Trek fan fiction special is imminent.

Page 8

THE PLAGUE CHRONICLES

Always look on the bright side of life!

If a train wreck or capsizing ship doesn't get you, then a flesh-eating bug will, according to this round up of virus paperbacks.

Page 24

PROSE AND CONS

Authors in lockdown!

Authors behind bars who earned money for cigarettes and protection by writing paperbacks.

Page 46

THE LOCKDOWN REVIEWS

Reviews from the other side!

Reviews from a group of paperback obsessives for whom quarantine with no social contact and only books for company is a way of life.

Page 54

GIL COHEN: ONE MAN ARMY

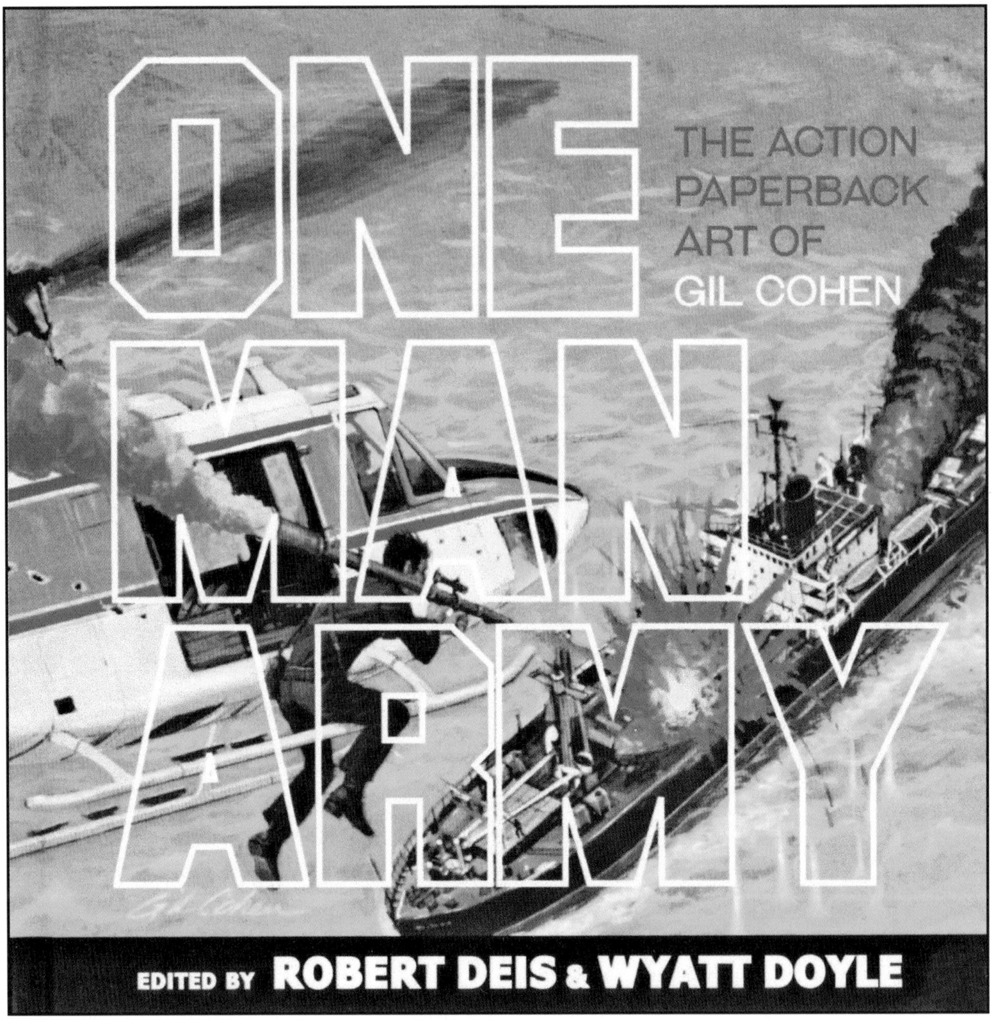

Occasionally an artist will produce the definitive portrayal of a character. The easier part is in matching their physical likeness to an author's description, but the true challenge is in capturing the essence of that fictional creation. This happens inevitably more often in comics than paperbacks, by their dint of being about recurring characters. However once in while, a paperback artist captures that lightning in a bottle.

Examples that's spring to mind are UK artist Richard Clifton-Dey who produced the definitive portrayal of western anti-hero Edge. James Bamas' visualisation of Doc Savage – with help from male model Steve Holland – is surely the one that pops up in your mind's eye at mention of that character's name. Perhaps Steranko, with his outstanding series of paintings for reissues of the Shadow?

And for any fan of men's action-adventure paperback, the name on the tip of your tongue is Gil Cohen, for his paintings of the long running Mack Bolan character and associated spin-offs. Cohen's work on these characters is celebrated in the hardcover **One-Man Army**, edited by Bob Deis and Wyatt Doyle and published under their New Texture imprint. Its title a clever word play on the Mack Bolan character, but also on Cohen's impressive ability to combine quantity and quality.

Gil Cohen

Weighing in at 155 full colour pages, the books consists of 100+ full page reproductions of Cohen's original artwork (sans titles and copy) which ran on paperback covers for **The Executioner**, **Mack Bolan**, **Able Team** and **Phoenix Force**, from 1969-89. It opens with a fascinating interview with Cohen, in which the artist discusses his use of friends rather than professionals as models, how he ended up moving with **The Executioner** when the series went from Pinnacle to Harlequin, and plenty of reflections on individual illustrations.

Reading Cohen's comments gave me a greater insight and appreciation for his work, especially his insistence upon correctly capturing how weapons were held by his characters. Despite not being interested in technical accuracy in escapist fiction, I was compelled to study this aspect of Cohen's work and admire his achievement.

Something else that I hadn't previously noticed was Cohen's ageing of Bolan, clearly showing the emergence of lines and wrinkles in images drawn in the 1980s, a logical aspect considering Bolan had been a veteran in the Vietnam War.

There were plenty of fascinating anecdotes in the interview, such as who was the real-life model for Bolan and that Cohen had unknowingly illustrated the first appearance of **The Executioner** - in a men's adventure mag - all of which were new to me. I will not ruin any surprises here.

Looking through the pages of **One-Man Army** you can see Cohen develop as a painter in three phases. The early Pinnacle book illustrations were much brighter in their colours, much more immediate and rawer in their execution, and their composition would typically include an attractive female sidekick. Then for the Harlequin/Gold Eagle re-boot of the series as **Mack Bolan**, the paintings became much more polished, the action much tighter and viewed through a closer lens focused on Bolan's pose and facial expression, with less in the way of backgrounds. Finishing with the team paintings, rendered with a photo-realism which is frighteningly good and requiring a technical expertise beyond mere mortals, but for me lacking the vitality of earlier paintings and betraying their origins in photo-reference.

Flicking through the pages again looking for which images to choose to illustrate this review, I am faced with a veritable one-man army of virtuoso paintings. For Bolan fanatics, all of the definitive covers are here, plus some new favourites. And like me, having read Cohen's words, you will have an even greater appreciation for his craft.

Order your copy of **One-Man Army** from Amazon and other on-line retailers.

JUSTIN MARRIOTT straps on his seat-belt, checks his oxygen mask and reads the safety brief as he does a health and safety assessment of mega-disaster paperbacks

DISASTER 70s!

With the advent of the blockbuster film, perhaps best typified by Jaws (1975), it was not just the boat that needed to be bigger in 70s pop-culture. Everything needed to be super-sized in cinema, TV and books, a trend started pre-Jaws by the disaster films The Poseidon Adventure (1972) and The Towering Inferno (1974).

Both of these genre-defining films were based on books - three to be exact- and from this point on, any example of modern technology, from ships, to planes, to amusement parks were transformed by a willing army of fictioneers into the most dangerous places on earth. Humans had survived any number of challenges thrown at them by nature and their Gods across the centuries, so how would they respond to their own technology malfunctioning and turning upon them?

Once I began to research the disaster novel, it soon became obvious that I needed to introduce some criteria for fear of being crushed by the resultant tower of books wobbling and collapsing on me. Most obviously I've kept the timeline to the era of the big-budget disaster film, from the early 70s through to the mid-80s.

I have also excluded ecological disaster novels dealing with natural phenomena such as famine, flood or drought, unless they were invoked by the greed of an avaricious businessman or scientific meddling. For instance, building a new town or hotel in the shadow of a failing dam, or creating a machine to change the weather would fit the bill.

I've also tended to exclude books that use a disaster as background to add additional drama – some of the works of John MacDonald spring to mind, such as **The Executioners** or **The Hurricane**, which are set against a back-drop of extreme weather, without being its raison d'etre. I have generally excluded Science Fiction, unless set in a believable near-future. And lastly, for reasons unknown to me, I also decided not to tackle the nuclear disaster novel.

So, if I were to try and label the books I have covered, it would be "man's folly resulting in a mega-disaster threatening the life of large groups". Hope that's cleared it up....

Before I discuss the story-lines, I would also like to mention their packaging. Perhaps it is because of their cross-over to the movies, and therefore posters, but the disaster paperbacks where the first body of books where I noticed the boundaries between logo and art disappearing. Now the title of the book might be made

Pan
THE TOWER
Richard Martin Stern
Coming soon as
IRWIN ALLEN'S
Production of
THE TOWERING INFERNO
A film based in part on this novel
A 20th CENTURY FOX-WARNER BROS. RELEASE

Pan
THE TOWER
Richard Martin Stern
See IRWIN ALLEN'S Production of
THE TOWERING INFERNO
A film based in part on this novel
A WARNER BROS. – 20th CENTURY-FOX RELEASE

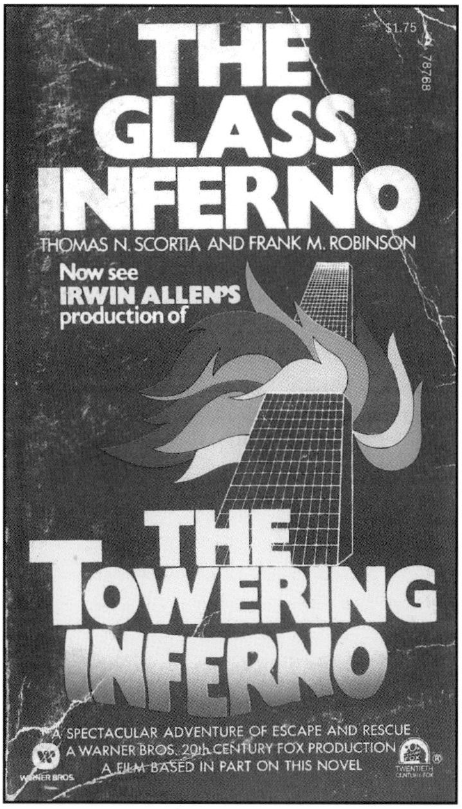
$1.75
78768
THE GLASS INFERNO
THOMAS N. SCORTIA AND FRANK M. ROBINSON
Now see
IRWIN ALLEN'S
production of
THE TOWERING INFERNO
A SPECTACULAR ADVENTURE OF ESCAPE AND RESCUE
A WARNER BROS. 20th CENTURY FOX PRODUCTION
A FILM BASED IN PART ON THIS NOVEL

CORONET
The most beautiful building in the world
becomes a raging furnace of death
THE GLASS INFERNO
Thomas N. Scortia & Frank M. Robinson

1971 reissue by Pan Books to tie-in to the movie adaptation which was a box-office smash.

The sequel was published after author Paul Gallico's death. The art is from the film poster.

up of crumbling bricks, or twisted metal, to thematically link with the cover painting. I've shown a selection of these on pages 12-13.

I'll start with Paul Gallico's book **The Poseidon Adventure** (1969) which became the inspiration for the entire vogue for disaster when it was adapted to film in 1972. In the famous story, a giant liner hosting a New Year's celebration is capsized by a tidal wave, and the survivors must claw their way through water-submerged corridors, red-hot metal and flash-fires to reach freedom through what was the bottom of the ship. Gallico's novel pulled the rug away from the feet of its readers by killing off key characters, but was dismissed as nothing more than a written-by-the-numbers thriller when first published. The film and its operatic depictions of death and destruction made it one of the highest-ever grossing films, so it was disasters-are-go as far as film studios and publishing houses were concerned.

Beyond the Poseidon Adventure (1978), was a follow-up but not published until two years after Gallico's death, so I wonder if it was posthumously finished by a ghost-writer. Set in the immediate aftermath of the survivors emerging, rumours that the stricken vessel contains gold bullion attracts a melting pot of pirates, war veterans and NY cops. Neither the book nor its film version drew much praise.

There are two boats in peril in **Storehouses of the Snow** (1980) by Edwin Woodward and Heather Bischoff, one a research ship and the other a luxury liner, as the world begins to disintegrate due to Antarctic ice sheets melting. But, perhaps wisely, there were few other books which emulated Poseidon's voyage (there had been a number of Titanic books, none better than 1955's **A Night to Remember** by Walter Lord). UK author John Wingate updated the premise in **The Sea Above Them** (1975) to a nuclear submarine stranded on the ocean floor, teetering on the edge of an oceanic cliff face and facing discovery by hostile Russians. This seems like such a great dramatic device, I am sure it must have also been used elsewhere.

1978 paperback which was part of a reprint series of Wingate's hardbacks by NEL, including Avalanche.

The Night Manhattan Burned aka The Pyromaniac's Guide to New York Landmarks.

There was another submarine disaster novel, this one being the world's first submarine oil tanker, which creates the titular **Spill!** (1979) having crashed into an iceberg whilst travelling from Alaska to Boston. Basil Jackson, author of **Spill!**, carved out quite the niche as an architect of disaster novels, most memorably with **The Night Manhattan Burned** (1979) in which a crippled super tanker limping to Staten Island harbour unleashes highly flammable gas. It reads like a pyromaniac's guide to NY landmarks.

The Deadly Frost (1979) by Terrence Moan peddled the same trick, but this time the holed tanker in Staten Island harbour leaks liquid methane gas into New York atmosphere. The final example of the oil-tanker disaster novels on my radar is **Firespill** (1977) by Ian Slater, where a huge slick from a collision catches fire just off the Canadian coast.

Beyond sea-vessels, disaster novels used other forms of transport, perhaps none more than the airplane, which was seeing huge growth in terms of tourism in the 70s and worldwide headlines with the launch of supersonic Concorde. Although not a disaster novel per se, Arthur Hailey's **Airport** (1968) became the literary runway for many aeronautical disaster novels and films. It inspired a series of films, two of which received tie-ins - **Airport 77** (1977) in which a luxurious plane loaded by a millionaire with treasures and his entourage crashes, and **Airport 80 – The Concorde** (1980) where the supersonic jet is menaced by a robot attack-plane.

Hailey had previously been credited as co-writer on **Flight into Danger** (1958), which John Castle wrote based on Hailey's script for a TV movie. Apparently, Hailey was so dissatisfied with Castle's approach that he began to write fiction. One of the most innovative, if not believable, stories was **Collision** (1974) by Spencer Dunmore, which has two giant jumbo-jets colliding mid-flight and becoming a Transformer style super-structure which is un-landable. Dunmore was an amateur pilot who specialised in aviation fiction, more typically focused on WW2 bomber-missions.

"ALL THE ELEMENTS OF A BESTSELLER ... BUILDS TO A CLIMAX OF SHOCKING INTENSITY STRONG ENOUGH TO SATISFY ANY READER!" —FT. WORTH STAR-TELEGRAM
CAT FIVE
ROBERT P. DAVIS
POCKET
82069-9
$1.95

SIGNET FILM SERIES • 451-Y6264 • $1.25
AN EVENT...
EARTHQUAKE
THE STORY OF A MOVIE
BY GEORGE FOX
SPECIAL! 24 PAGES OF SENSATIONAL PHOTOS!

BT
50865
CDC
$1.50
David James
FOREST FIRE
MAN'S GREATEST ALLY UNCHECKED – BECOMES HIS DEADLIEST ENEMY

MANOR BOOKS 12287 ★ $1.25
TRAIN WRECK
JEREMIAH JACK

MANOR BOOKS 12290 ★ $1.25
CYCLONE
ERIC NILSEN

LB
271DK
$1.50
MARTIN WALLACE TYLER
DEATH WAS RUSHING TOWARD
THEM. THEIR WHOLE WORLD
WOULD END WITHIN HOURS.

BT
50845
CDC
$1.50
BLIZZARD
DAVID JAMES

A THRILLING
NOVEL.
A MAJOR
MOTION
PICTURE.
AVALANCHE

Pan
NOW A MAJOR MOTION PICTURE FROM UNIVERSAL
AIRPORT '77
A NOVEL BY
MICHAEL SCHEFF & DAVID SPECTOR
BASED UPON THEIR SCREENPLAY
STORY BY
H.A.L. CRAIG & CHARLES KUENSTLE
INSPIRED BY THE NOVEL AIRPORT BY ARTHUR HAILEY.

Pan
IS THE FIRST AMERICAN CONCORDE DOOMED BY A ROBOT KILLER PLANE?
AIRPORT '80
THE CONCORDE
A NOVEL BY KERRY STEWART
BASED ON A SCREENPLAY BY ERIC ROTH
FROM A STORY BY JENNINGS LANG
INSPIRED BY THE NOVEL AIRPORT BY ARTHUR HAILEY
NOW A FILM OF SKY-HIGH SUSPENSE FROM UNIVERSAL

Pan
SPENCER DUNMORE
COLLISION
'Breathtaking . . . will make your blood run cold'
DAILY MIRROR

Pan
JOHN CASTLE &
ARTHUR HAILEY
FLIGHT INTO DANGER

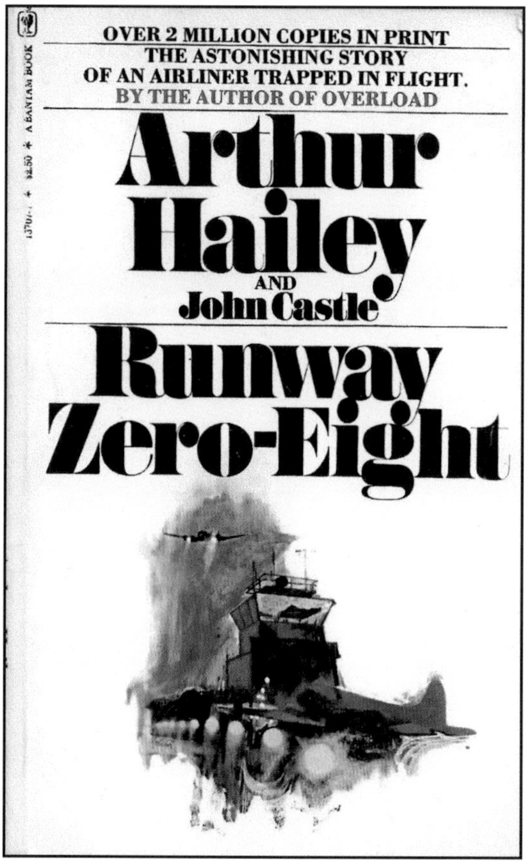

First published in 1958, by 1979 - according to the copyright indicia - this title had one through 31 printings!

UK 1977 reprint of 1974's Jet Stream, referencing a made-for-TV adaptation which probably never aired in the UK.

Supersonic (1975) by Basil Jackson (him again) was a look at a Concorde where pretty much everything that could go wrong, does – Jackson is both a pessimist and does his research - leaving the passengers with a grim outlook. Jackson would write more aeronautical novels, including **Flameout** (1976) which combines an air-disaster with a conspiracy thriller. More MACH-1 hi-jinks abounded in **Flight One** (1972) where America's first supersonic aircraft, The Screaming Aardvark, takes off on its maiden flight with a plane full of trouble. First-time author Charles Carpentier was a director of aerospace information films, so the book is full of technical verisimilitude as well as soap operatics.

Flying at a lower altitude was **Jet Stream** (1973) by Austin Ferguson, which went on to be filmed as **Mayday 40,000 feet!** and combines two weary pilots who are flying into one of the worst blizzards in memory and a dangerous prisoner wreaking havoc on board.

Talkdown (1979) by Brian LeComber, has an incapacitated pilot meaning a female passenger must take the wings down. LeComber, an ex-aerobatic flyer only wrote three books and quit as apparently he found the process of writing "bloody boring!"

Star Struck (1975) by Ernest (**Shaft**) Tidyman, combined the airplane and large building disaster sub-genres, by crashing a private plane into the side of the Empire State building and trapping the passengers in the crumbling wreckage, high over the NY streets.

Switching to trains whose high speed and automation were ample material for a disaster in the minds of authors. **Crash!** (1975) by James Broom Lynne, who also wrote as James Quatermain, had first been published as **The Commuters** (1973) but had been given a swift make-over by Pan Books in the UK. This was a more representative title, as the book is more focused on the characters populating the train than its climatic crash. **Wreck** (1977) by Parley J Cooper adheres to the disaster-movie formula of mis-matched strangers with a variety of motives thrown into uneasy alliance in order to escape.

Bullet Train (1980) was a collaboration between Joseph Rance and Arei Kato set around the Japanese uber-fast transportation, in which terrorists will set off a bomb if the speed drops below 50mph. Fans of 90s action movies may recognise this plot device! Robert Byrne explored **The Tunnel** (1977) in which a new underwater railway tunnel linking England and France is bombed by terrorists.

Away from transport, let us revisit **The Towering Inferno**, which in 1974 was a highly successful film and cemented the trend for disaster culture started by **The Poseidon Adventure**. It was based on two separate books, **The Tower** (1973) by Richard Martin Stern and **The Glass Inferno** (1974) by Thomas N Scortia and Frank M Robinson. Apparently both were optioned for filming, but in a rare outbreak of common sense in the film industry, Warner Bros and 20th Century Fox studios agreed to make one film rather than a competing pair. The book **Tower** was more of a psychological thriller showing how the residents of a 125-story NY skyscraper react as their celebratory opening party is overtaken by flames. Whereas **Inferno** was much more focused on the technical detail of how a fire could spread across a 66-storey Chicago block.

I am not aware of any other sky-scraper disaster books, but I must mention **Nothing Lasts Forever** (1979) by Roderick Thorp from which the classic movie **Die Hard** took its inspiration and J G Ballard's **High Rise** (1975) in which an architect has intentionally designed a building to induce psychosis amongst its residents.

There were many novels dealing with the extreme ebb and flow of the oceans, although they are typically driven by ecological systems rather than man's folly. So I have excluded many potential candidates for inclusion, such as **Goodbye Piccadilly** (1980) an interesting setting of a detective story in a flooded London, **The Day the Oceans Overflowed** (1964) by Charles Fontenay, **Deluge** (1976) by Richard Doyle which depicted the impact of a flood which would not happen now due to the construction of the Thames Flood Barrier, and **Tidal Wave** (1975) by Martin Wallace where a natural wave threatens Hawaii.

I can warn you about **Flood** (1979) by Richard Martin Stern of **The Tower (ing Inferno)** fame, in which greedy entrepreneurs looking to build a prosperous new town ignore the precarious nature of a dam which when previously breached had submerged a town in the late nineteenth century. I can provide a ride with **The Fifth Horseman** (1976) by Walter Harris in which drilling for oil in the North Sea causes the seabed to collapse, which triggers a

"Let the train take the strain" was the strap-line used by British Rail for their TV advertising for many years! Crash! Was a retitled version of The Commuters focused on the ensemble of characters trapped on board, a familiar model followed by Wreck. Bullet Train was possibly the inspiration for one of the most successful action movies of the 1990s.

RICHARD MARTIN STERN
Best-selling author of SNOWBOUND SIX, THE WILL and THE TOWER
Flood
A DISASTER THAT COULD HAPPEN!

THE HEARTSTOPPING NOVEL OF A CITY FACING DISASTER
BY RICHARD DOYLE
AUTHOR OF IMPERIAL 109
DELUGE

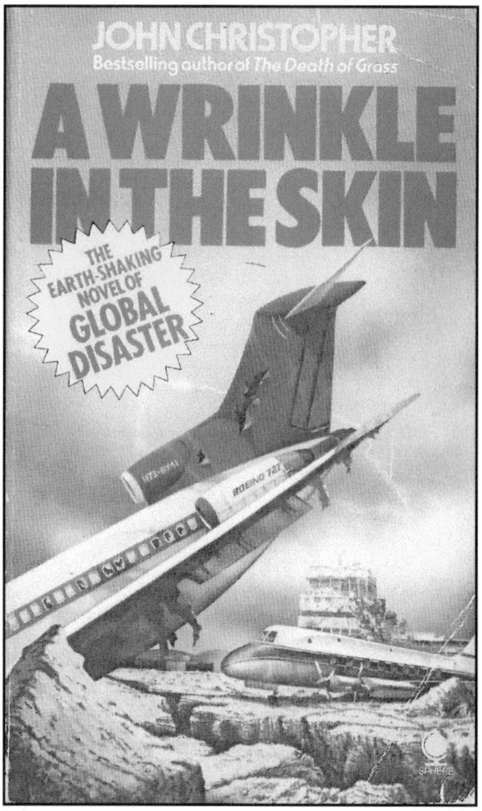
JOHN CHRISTOPHER
Bestselling author of The Death of Grass
A WRINKLE IN THE SKIN
THE EARTH-SHAKING NOVEL OF GLOBAL DISASTER
BOEING 727
SPHERE

A shattering novel of the world's greatest catastrophe
THE FIFTH HORSEMAN
Walter Harris
586 04388 8
Panther

MAGNUM
TOM BARLING
GOODBYE PICCADILLY
'TERRIFYING AND COMPELLING'
CINZ
FUJI FIL
TOM BARLING'S
BESTSELLING BLOCKBUSTER OF
THE DROWNING OF LONDON

Deadly weather novels! Death Cloud descended from science journalist Michael Mannion.

More clouds of doom, this time from Thomas Page with a tale of a sentient storm versus meddling boffins.

flood which submerges half of England. The hero scientist who fights his way across a primal Britain is typical of the heroes in John Christopher's many eco-disaster books such as **Wrinkle in the Skin** (1965), from which this book is heavily derived.

In **Denver is Missing** (1971) by D.F. Jones, drilling operations in the Pacific Ocean hit a large pocket of gas. It turns out that the gas is nitrogen and when it drains enough, the ocean collapses into the void, breaking open an even larger pocket. This pocket explodes in dramatic fashion, sending tidal waves all over the Pacific basin.

There was a raft of extreme water weather books, but the only I am aware of which falls into 'mans' folly' criteria was Thomas Page's **Sigmet Active** (1978) a batty story of how the US military's experiments destroy part of the ozone layer, which responds by creating a sentient storm which kills off the meddling scientists one by one. I am aware of a paperback from that same year called **Weather War** (1978) but I do not own a copy. On-line sources, and the title, suggest it is about a plot to trigger WW3 through a series of weather strikes.

There was also **Death Cloud** (1976) by Michael Mannion, but this was just a run-of-the-mill non-intelligent killer cloud title. The sound-a-like **Doom Wind** (1986) by Max Gunther featured 300 miles per hour gusts created by a passing comet, menacing all of the standard characters in settings for a competent disaster thriller. **Mists of Fear** (1955) was yet another John Creasey book featuring his quasi occult detective, Dr Palfrey, who investigates the source of a mist that seemingly consumes its victims.

Books considered but excluded are **Vortex** (1978) by Australian author Jon Cleary about the impact of a hurricane on a Missouri town, **Hurricane** (1976) an archetypal nature-wreaks-havoc-on-

Opposite page- clever packaging on this detective meets disaster novel, with the cover image painted to look as if the book's pages have dried out having been immersed.

beautiful-people pot-boiler by famous comics writer Gardner Fox and **Condominium** (1977), John D MacDonald's railing call against the commercial exploitation of his home state Florida. Name-checking both **Towering Inferno** and **Earthquake** was **Slide** (1976) by Gerald A Browne where excessive rain creates a mud-slide which traps people in a Californian supermarket.

With the massive success of **Star Wars** it seemed obvious that popular culture would introduce elements of science-fiction into the disaster novel. Although falling outside of the 'man's folly' angle, there was something about the earth being hit by a space-rock that seems very 70s disaster to me, and created a small body of films and books.

I recollect that the film **Meteor** (1979) was advertised seemingly everywhere at the time, and it included a tie-in paperback by Franklin Coen based on Edmund H. North's screen-play, which in itself was inspired by a paper written by MIT students the previous decade. Beating both the film and book to the punch was **A Fire in the Sky** (1978) which was a TV movie about a giant comet heading for Earth and had its own tie-in. The original story was by Paul (**The Poseidon Adventure**) Gallico.

There were several other space-rock books that landed around the same time as **Meteor**, such as **The Hermes Fall** (1978) by Australian John Baxter. Perhaps too much SF to warrant inclusion, it is delightfully tacky and pulpy if you like that sort of thing. **Impact!** (1979) by R. Fodor and G Taylor mixed a Cold War theme as Japan, Russia and America move into World War Three following a series of asteroid collisions. **Shiva Descending** (1980) by Gregory Benford and William Rotsler has an asteroid the size of a mountain about to hit the Earth and wipe out all life.

There was also a shower of connected titles that I don't own and doubt if I will ever feel true fulfilment

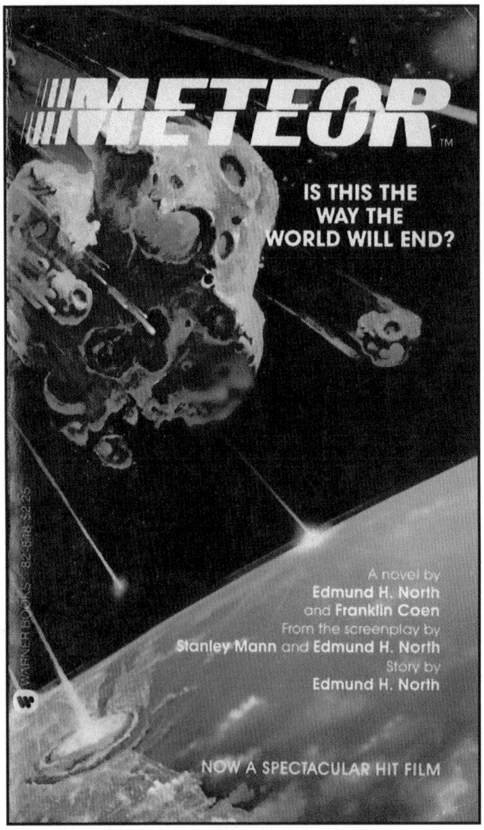

***Slide** - budgets typically precluded original photos being shot for mega-disaster novels, but this is a rare and effective example. The font design is also a clever play on the title.*

***Meteor** - the film and its tie-in heralded a storm of giant rocks landing on a town near you.*

***Opposite page** - The Year of the Comet was repackaged by Sphere, along with a number of John Christopher novels, to ride the disaster craze.*

Jon Cleary's excellent earthquake adventure Fall of the Eagle received a 1970's cover make-over from Richard Clifton-Dey.

Impact was one of the shower of asteroid cash-ins that descended on the late 1970s

Quaking Terror - as well as being a truly terrible pun - was one of a small number of men's adventure books featuring villains wielding earthquake machines. Cover by George Wilson.

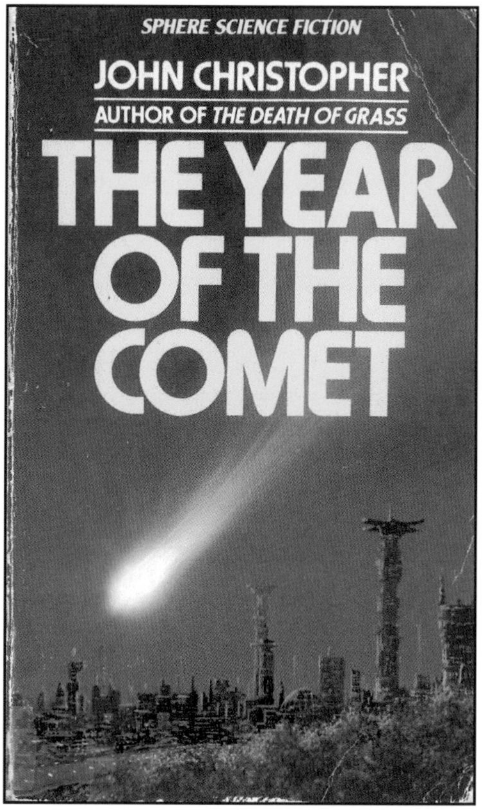
SPHERE SCIENCE FICTION
JOHN CHRISTOPHER
AUTHOR OF THE DEATH OF GRASS
THE YEAR OF THE COMET

THE FALL OF AN EAGLE
JON CLEARY
'Jon Cleary belongs with Steinbeck and O'Hara'
Gavin Lyall, Sunday Times
FONTANA

LB
648 • $1.95
A GIGANTIC METEOR HURTLES THROUGH SPACE TOWARD A HEAD-ON COLLISION WITH EARTH!
IMPACT!
R.V. FODOR AND G.J. TAYLOR

THE GREAT ACTION-PACKED SERIES WITH OVER 5 MILLION IN PRINT!
No. 45
MARK HARDIN IS THE
PENETRATOR
QUAKING TERROR
by Lionel Derrick
If the Penetrator doesn't stop him a madman will take the nation by storm!

until I do. **Gargantua** (1977) by Anthony Coburn promises "20 billion tons of destruction hurtling towards the Earth." From publishers on the lower-rung, Major Books provided **Meteorite Track 291** by Gary Paulsen which has a meteorite streaking towards the heart of America and **The Meteroic Affair** (1982) by Joseph Tabler landed courtesy of the crap-tastic Carousel Books. **Fireball** by Vic Mayhew and Doug Long (1979) has a blazing planetoid on crash collision with Earth in eight days.

Comet (1985) from Robert Charles is another one I have dodged, in which Hailey's Comet brings with it a cloud of interstellar dust which blocks out the sun. The on-line synopsis made me think of Colin Wilson's **Space Vampires** (1976) where the outer-space parasites hitched a ride on Hailey's Comet. John Christopher's **The Year of the Comet** (1955) was re-released in 1978 when the space-rock genre was biggest, despite not being directly related to such matter.

Unlike **Meteor**, which made little impact at the box-office, the earlier **Earthquake** (1974), which very much fell into the disaster-suspense category, was a real smash thanks to its cutting-edge special effects. The paperback tie-in was merely a reprint of the screenplay with a large gallery of stills showing LA in ruins. However, it and its imitators, typically focused on the San Andreas fault, and did not feature any 'man's folly' angle. If you are looking for a recommendation for a book to make the earth move, I point you towards **The Fall of an Eagle** (1964) by Jon Cleary which combines adventure and romance during a Turkish earthquake.

There were at least two men's adventure series which featured villains using technology to create quakes or volcanoes. In **The Penetrator 45, Quaking Terror** (1982) by Lionel Derrick, Mount St Helens, Mount Baker and the whole Pacific coast go up in flame and molten lava, with arch-villain and suspected vampire Magarac to blame. **The Destroyer 5; Dr Quake** (1972) has an earthquake creating machine stolen and used to hold America to ransom, relayed in the always amusing and entertaining style you might associate with the series.

The long-running Nick Carter spy series must have used every dramatic device available to a deadline-plagued author, so unsurprisingly there were two quake related entries. In **Earth Shaker** (1982) by Robert E. Vardeman, the crazed scientist is warming up on other countries to perfect his quake before turning to the US. **The Q-Man** (1981) written by John Stevenson, has the titular renegade reducing San Diego to dust and threatening to spread the artificially triggered earth tremors along the Californian coast.

California is a huge magnet to tourists, and as attractions competed to be the biggest and the tallest, they came to the attention of the disaster fictioneers. **Roller Coaster** (1977) was a Burton Wohl adaptation of a screenplay for the George Segal movie in which an extortionist demands a million dollars or he will continue to sabotage the titular thrill-ride. **Amusement Park** (1977) by Robert Stuart Nathan has the Sky Chariot, billed as the world's largest attraction, enveloped by fire set by a mad arsonist.

Snow or icebound thrillers are lined up for a study of their own in a future issue, but with regards to the 'man's folly' disaster angle, the one that leapt to mind was Robert Weverka's movie tie-in to **Avalanche** (1978), where developers ignore warnings in building a luxurious lodge in the mountains with predictable results.

Sub-Zero! (1979) by Robert Walker, is set in the then near-future of 2000, where meddling with the weather has ushered in a new ice-age, and a news team are stalked in an ice-bound skyscraper by a killer. Its premise is reminiscent of Brian Coffey's (Dean Koontz) **The Face of Fear** (1977) in which a psychic mountaineer faces-off against a serial killer in a sky-scraper set finale. Another SF-related account of deadly snowfall was from John Boland, who forecast a **White August** (1955), in which radioactive snow is dumped on Britain, with the key suspect a renegade Austrian scientist.

There was also a snow-as-weapon novel, **Freeze** (1977, later renamed **Blizzard**) by George Stone, in which a hawkish submarine commander uses his craft's nuclear sub-reactors to create a permanent snowstorm. Of course, it works far better than he might have ever guessed, and soon the disastrously intense blizzard covers America, and by the conclusion is surrounding the Eiffel Tower. It was soon followed by **Sunstrike** (1978) by George Carpozi where a scientist blocks the sun rays and ushers in a new ice-age.

Please write into **The Paperback Fanatic** with any other books in this genre and I will run them in future issues.

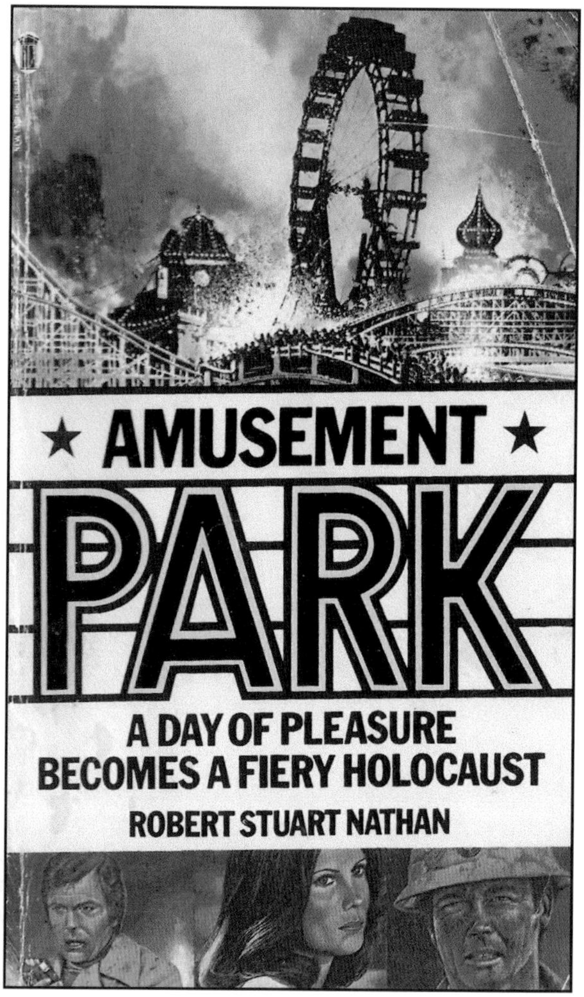

Amusement Park - a cinematic treatment from cover artist David McAllister who often used panels or strips to suggest a film connection. It looks as if he used actors John Saxon and Roger Moore for photo-reference.

Roller Coaster - Burton Wohl's movie tie-in had an excellent cover which was lifted from the film's poster.

Freeze - the retitled Blizzard trumpeted that this wasn't just a thriller, it was a "superthriller" which sums up the hyperbole of the disaster genre.

JUSTIN MARRIOTT looks at the fictional viruses, plagues and lurgies which infected popular fiction in the 1960s and 70s.

THE PLAGUE CHRONICLES

Wikipedia tells me that the second half of the 20th Century was a golden age for the virus, with over 2,000 varieties discovered. Based on a cursory glance through my bookshelves, I imagine there were nearly as many fictional viruses created by publishers and authors during that same period.

As far back as the 1930s, Fu Manchu would regularly cook up test tubes of virulent germs, or entire cities would be ravaged by fatal plagues in the pages of The Spider. But the threat of an intentionally released virus really spread with the surge in spy thrillers during the 1960s, which then continued into the men's adventure genre of the 1970s, where the conveyor-belt nature of the series characters inevitably had their busy authors recycling such themes.

Inspired by the space-race of the 1960s, science-fiction explored the impact of viruses inadvertently bought back to Earth. (Plot-spoiler – it is not good news.) More brain than brawn were the doctors starring in a line of medical thrillers during the 1970s, recast as heroes as they race to cure a deadly disease, sometimes based on actual outbreaks in true "ripped from the headlines" style. In the 1980s, horror welcomed the virus as a great excuse to write about outbreaks of psychotic violence or to describe an especially disgusting pus-dripping boil.

I am sure that it comes as no great surprise, but the virus/plague genre is not a cheery one, and unusually for popular fiction, the principal characters are as likely to face an uncertain future or imminent death as discover a miraculous cure for the disease. Take for instance **Plague** (1978), a door-stopper of a 400 page thriller unleashed by Graham Masterton, in which a father and daughter travel across an America destroyed by an unnamed super-virus. Anyone expecting a cosy beach-read may well be shocked at Masterton's explicit sex and violence as moral codes disintegrate as the disease takes hold.

Masterton more typically operates in the straight horror arena, conjuring up **Night Plague** (1991), a typically engrossing and skilfully constructed shocker, in which an AIDs like virus is given to a musician in London, as part of a supernatural plot to destroy the world. Less effective is his early Lovecraftian horror, **The**

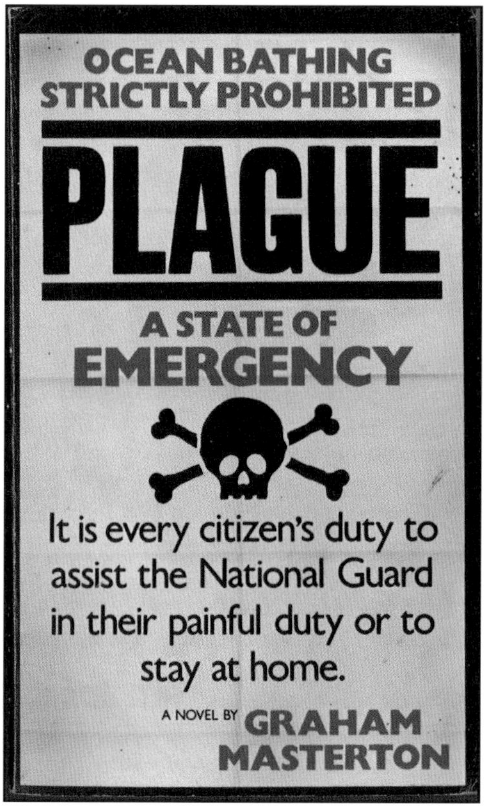
OCEAN BATHING
STRICTLY PROHIBITED
PLAGUE
A STATE OF
EMERGENCY
It is every citizen's duty to assist the National Guard in their painful duty or to stay at home.
A NOVEL BY GRAHAM MASTERTON

author of Night Warriors and Death Dream
GRAHAM MASTERTON
"[It] will give you all the nightmare material you require!"
– West Coast Review of Books on Death Dream
NIGHT PLAGUE
TOR HORROR

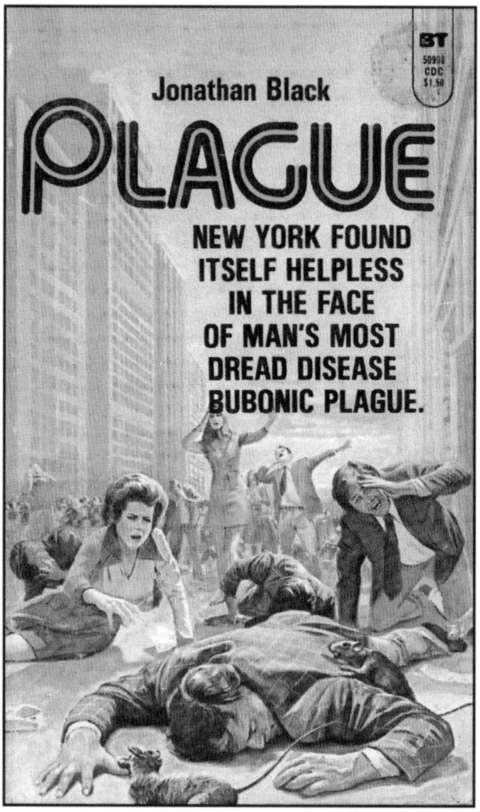
BT
Jonathan Black
PLAGUE
NEW YORK FOUND ITSELF HELPLESS IN THE FACE OF MAN'S MOST DREAD DISEASE BUBONIC PLAGUE.

The Witches
SPHERE
Death, degradation and damnation were their trademark!
8: THE PLAGUE
James Darke
A Sphere adult series

Wells of Hell (1979), where drinking the local water changes the townspeople into crustacean shamblers, which reminded me of a classic Basil Wolverton comic strip.

Another **Plague** (1976) originated from Jonathan Black, detailing an outbreak of the bubonic plague in New York in an especially unmemorable novel for lower-rung publisher Belmont Tower. Big on descriptions of pus-leaking boils and extracts from medical journals, light on characterisation, plot and drama. Frank G Slaughter had already unleashed an **Epidemic!** (1961) of plague-ridden rats on Manhattan, mixing Cold War intrigue and a romantic triangle in his commercial style.

The Plague (1986) was also the title in the eighth and final entry to **The Witches** series by James Darke (Laurence James). Although it kicks-off with the arrival of bubonic plague carrying rats in seventeenth century England, it is more concerned about the kinky sex to be derived from a witch-finding theme. And kinky it most certainly is, with a priest-hating, priapic dwarf taking centre-stage.

A much more effective use of the plague was in **The Black Death** (1977), with fleabites starting an outbreak in New York. Authors Gwynneth Cravens and John Marr effectively combine compelling and believable medical detail with a suitably grungy portrayal of 70s era Big Apple. There was another **Black Death** (1988), of the **Paperbacks from Hell** strain, with a flesh-eating bug inadvertently released from a north Indiana graveyard, which turns into mush the flesh of anyone contracting it.

A clever use of plague-carrying rodents in a period setting can be found in **The Holmes-Dracula File** (1978), part of a ten-book series by Fred Saberhagen, where a mad killer is planning to release the creatures during Queen Victoria's Jubilee celebrations. A clever twist on the legendary untold Holmes story **The Giant Rat of Sumatra**, this is a rollicking good read.

Death in Yellow (1981), book 31 of men's adventure series **The Butcher**, has a breed of plague carrying super rats with razor fangs about to be unleashed from the sewers by a stereotypical 'Yellow Peril' style villain. One of the longer-running men's adventure series, The Butcher features a government agent granted impunity to use lethal force, which appeared under the house name Stuart Jason. In this case Michael Avallone was behind the typewriter and it is typical of his output.

Long-running James Bond knock-off Nick Carter evaded the **Strike of the Hawk** (1980) by Joseph L Gilmore which starts off with Carter stopping the bubonic plague being unleashed by terrorist group NOTCH. I don't own a copy of **The Creeping Plague** (1963) by Richard MacGregor

Epidemic! By Frank Slaughter has gone through multiple editions. Here is the US first paperback edition from Pocket Books.

The Black Death is not a New York crushed by giant rat book. The world still awaits with baited breath.

from UK mushroom publisher Digit, but based on its cover illustration of a large brown rat and title, I assume it is a card-carrying member of the plague club. Definitely not, is **The Hamelin Plague** (1963) by A Bertam Chandler, a typically shoddy Monarch book about an alien invasion by intelligent rat mutants.

There are no scaly creatures to be found in **A Plague of Dragons** (1965) by John Michael Brett (Miles Tripp), the second in a Hugo Baron trilogy, one of the many spy characters launched in the wake of James Bond. Baron's mission is to investigate a mysterious Chinese *nyr* organisation whose new leader Dr Kwang is developing the latest in germ warfare.

The Eleventh Plague (1973) is a compact and gripping thriller, in which a highly contagious and deadly form of pneumonia sweeps across America. Credited author L T Peters is claimed to be a pseudonym for a husband/wife writing team, with the husband being a doctor specialising in infectious diseases. I learned a long time ago not to believe any author biography, but the science seems credible and the hero is a doctor with a brain the size of a planet rather than biceps the size of a water-melon, so it could be accurate.

A Plague of Sailors (1971) has a ship bound for Israel with relief supplies for earthquake victims rammed by terrorists, and its load of eight thousand tons of grain infected with Anthrax. Writer Brian Callison specialised in nautical thrillers with great aplomb, and this story featuring Brevet Cable, his unorthodox merchant seaman, is another well-crafted and exciting example of his craft.

The White Plague (1982) by Frank Herbert was an excellent genre mash-up from the author of **Dune**, in which a bacteriologist, driven insane by the death of his family in a terrorist attack, releases a deadly virus in the three countries he holds responsible.

There were four **Outbreaks** that I know of. The first **Outbreak** (1968) mixes medical and kidnap sub-genres, as a doctor tasked with containing an outbreak of smallpox carried into the United Kingdom by a now dead counterfeiter and his missing wife. When organised crime become involved, the doctor finds the lives of his family threatened. Author Lionel Black (Dudley Barker) is part of the generation of British thriller writers who are mostly forgotten, despite producing highly readable and competently crafted books such as this.

1978 Ace edition of the Dracula and Sherlock Holmes team up with a painting by Robert Adragna

Death in Yellow takes place in "an underground complex ruled by a demonic Chinaman .... and a well-endowed relentlessly cruel nymphomaniac." As depicted by Fred Love.

In a similar vein is Elleston Trevor, whose **The Pillars of Midnight** (1957) was still being reprinted in the 1970s, a characteristically taut and well-constructed account of a smallpox epidemic, with a focus on one hospital.

Outbreak (1978) chronicled an outbreak of Legionnaire's disease in a convention hotel, written for commercial reasons by English professor Robert Di Maria, who had enjoyed critical success but was broke. There had been an actual break-out of legionnaires at a convention hotel in Philadelphia in 1976, so publishers were actively seeking out books on this theme.

The third **Outbreak** (1987) was by Robin Cook which was one of his medical-thrillers, and I am aware of a fourth **Outbreak** by Ruth Marianne (1977), but I have not seen a copy.

That same year, Thomas Scortia and Frank Robinson, the giants of disaster-lit through their book **The Glass Inferno** (1974), unleashed Legionnaire's disease in a veteran's convention, in **The Nightmare Factor** (1978), which also spring boarded on the same events as **Outbreak**. It echoes the infamous CIA MKUltra trials of feeding LSD to the unwitting, and the pair know how to produce a slick and thought-provoking thriller.

The Ringway Virus (1976) was a commercially successful novel for publishers New English Library, in which a new fatal strain of influenza leaves the population facing an impossible choice between isolation or reproduction. More melodrama and travelog than thriller, the second half of the book is set in a colourful Australia, which is where Russell Foreman originated.

One by One (1965) has London swept by plague during a sweltering July, and focuses more on social satire and commentary than adrenalized thrills, following a veterinarian conscripted into the front line of virus defence and his wife who is seven months pregnant. This was the downbeat and chilling first novel by Penelope Gilliatt, who was more successful as a film critic and Oscar-winning screenplay writer.

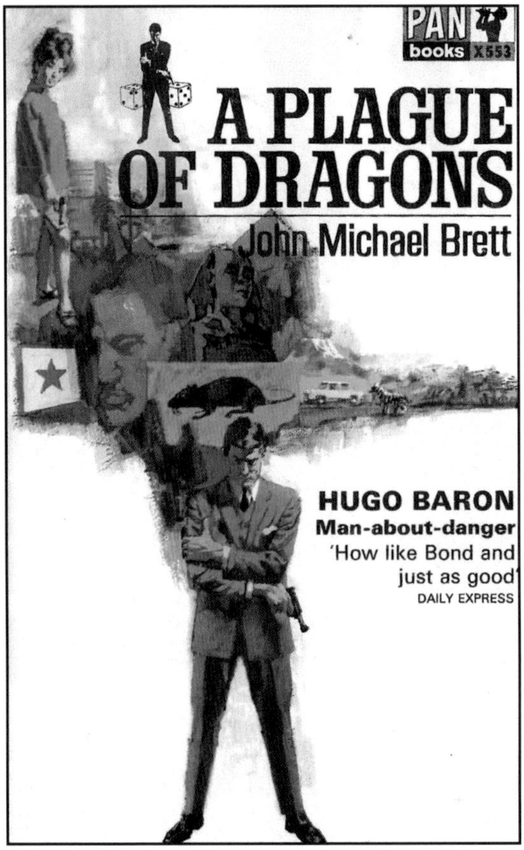

A Plague of Dragons was the second in a solid yet short-lived spy series by Miles Tripp as John Michael Brett.

1976 Mayflower paperback edition of the 1974 novel, written under the pseudonym of L T Peters.

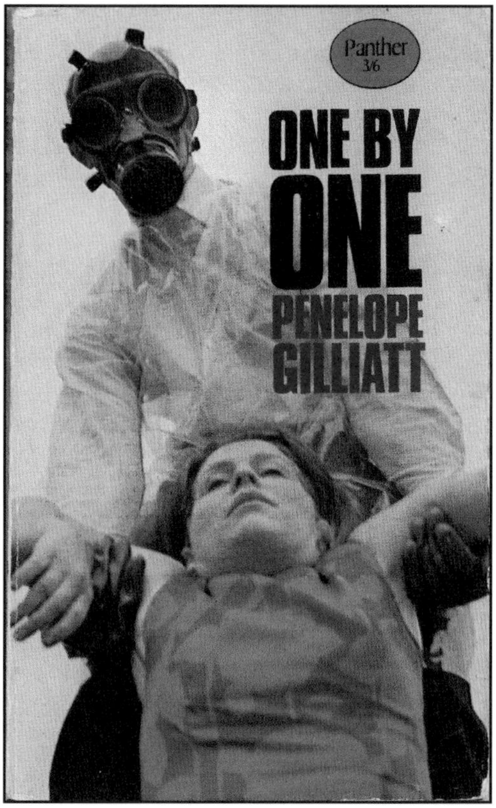
Panther
3/6
ONE BY
ONE
PENELOPE
GILLIATT

CORONET
AUTHOR OF THE VOYEUR
VECTOR
Only the great storytelling magnetism of a Henry Sutton
could get this powerful and gripping theme across
in the way that it deserves
U.S. ARMY
15TH A.M.CORPS

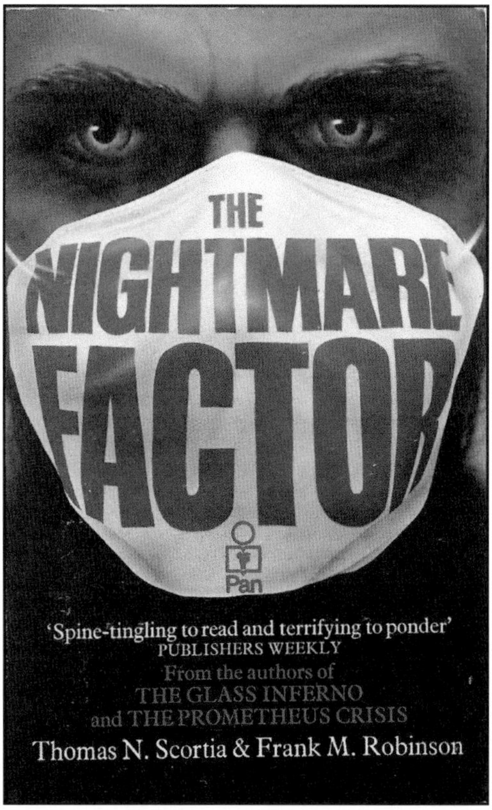
THE
NIGHTMARE
FACTOR
Pan
'Spine-tingling to read and terrifying to ponder'
PUBLISHERS WEEKLY
From the authors of
THE GLASS INFERNO
and THE PROMETHEUS CRISIS
Thomas N. Scortia & Frank M. Robinson

NEW ENGLISH LIBRARY
From the author of 'The Paragon'
ELLESTON
TREVOR
THE PILLARS
OF MIDNIGHT
GAZETTE
EPIDEMIC
DEATH
TOLL

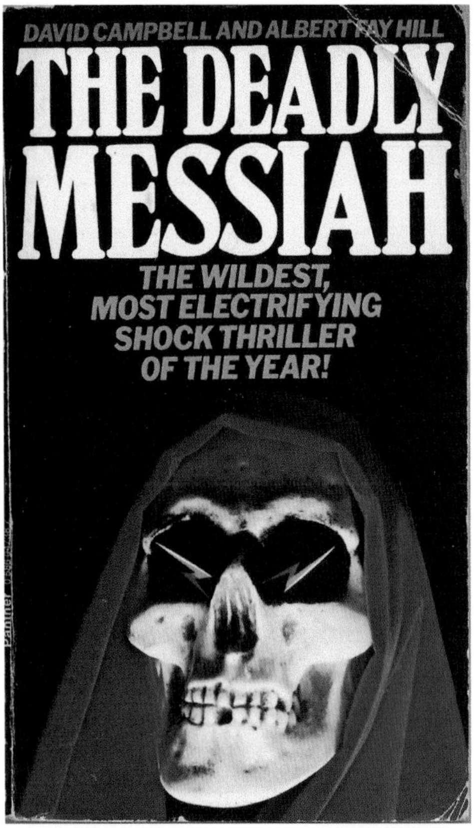

Darkest of Nights (1962) was another early look at the impact of a deadly virus on the social and political landscape, with Charles Eric Maine (David McIlwain) providing a look through the eyes of his hero, a reporter who makes many sacrifices to uncover the truth and ensure the safety of his family. Maine's SF books from the 60s were retitled in the following decade to fit in with the trend of block-busters, so this book became **The Big Death** and his **The Tide Went Out** (1958) turned into **Thirst**.

Inoculate (1979) by Neil Bayne was a no-frills and no-thrills conspiracy novel where the only scientist who knows the cure for a worldwide plague is kidnapped. On the less conventional side of the virus thriller, **The Deadly Messiah** (1976) by David Campbell and Albert Fay Hill, it's not a doctor that solves the mystery of a fatal disease that devastates a small Kentucky town, but an astrologist, who acts as an early proponent of **Mindhunter** style FBI profiling.

Also left-field, but intentionally so, was **The Droop** (1971) a slim and rough-hewn book with a sexy core that cashed in on topical themes. It was typical output from New English Library, and possibly a response to the growth of women's liberation at that time, as the book portrays a world where 95% of the Britain's men contract a virus which renders them impotent. Silly and throwaway, albeit cleverly written, I note that no other books by Rosse appeared. New English Library editor Mark Howell once mentioned it was his favourite book, so I wonder if he had a hand in it.

Science-fiction relatives to **The Droop** included **World Without Men** by Charles Eric Maine (1958) which is a thought-provoking and intelligent and **World Without Women** (1960) by Day Keene and Leonard Pruyn, which is not thought-provoking or intelligent. But great fun.

Similar themes were prevalent in **The Man From T.O.M.C.A.T.** series by Mallory T Knight (Bernhardt Hurwood), which was part of the sexy spy genre of the 60s. In **The Dirty Rotten Depriving Ray** (1967), the series' yellow peril villain Wang is developing a beam that deprives men of the ability to make love while still leaving

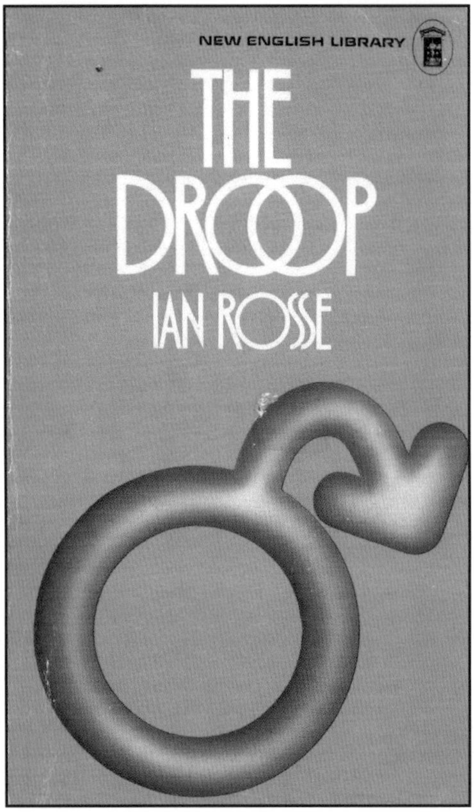

In The Deadly Messiah there is only one solution - send in the astrologists!

The Droop was the only novel by Ian Rosse, whom I suspect was a member of the publisher's editorial staff.

Opposite page

World Without Men was one of Gold Medal's rare excursions into SF territory courtesy of the sex-mad Day Keene.

The Ring-A-Ding UFOs was one of the four-episode female sexy spy series from Big Bob Tralins.

The Big Death was a revised version of The Darkest of Nights.

A dynamic cover for a later US edition of The Satan Bug which had originally been published under the Ian Stuart pseudonym.

GOLD MEDAL L1504
45¢
GOLD MEDAL SCIENCE-FICTION CLASSIC
WORLD WITHOUT WOMEN
The scourge had spread all over earth—killing all but a few women, for whose favors the price was Death
by DAY KEENE and LEONARD PRUYN

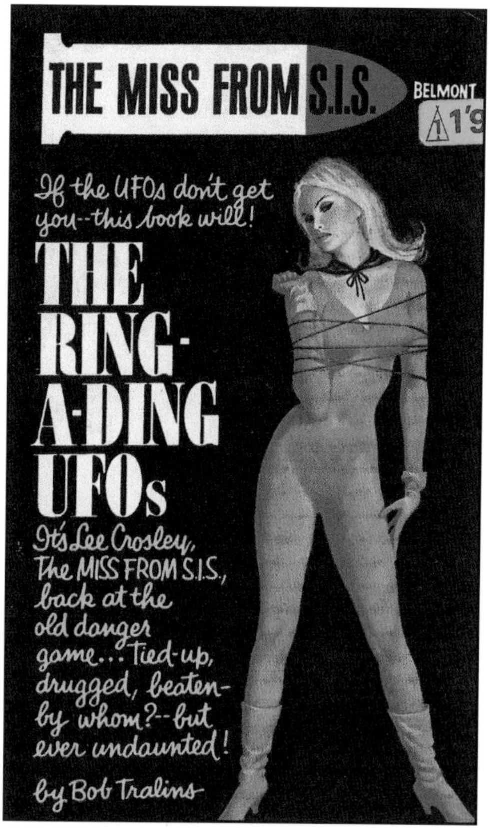
THE MISS FROM S.I.S.
BELMONT
1'9
If the UFOs don't get you--this book will!
THE RING-A-DING UFOs
It's Lee Crosley, The MISS FROM S.I.S., back at the old danger game... Tied-up, drugged, beaten-by whom?--but ever undaunted!
by Bob Tralins

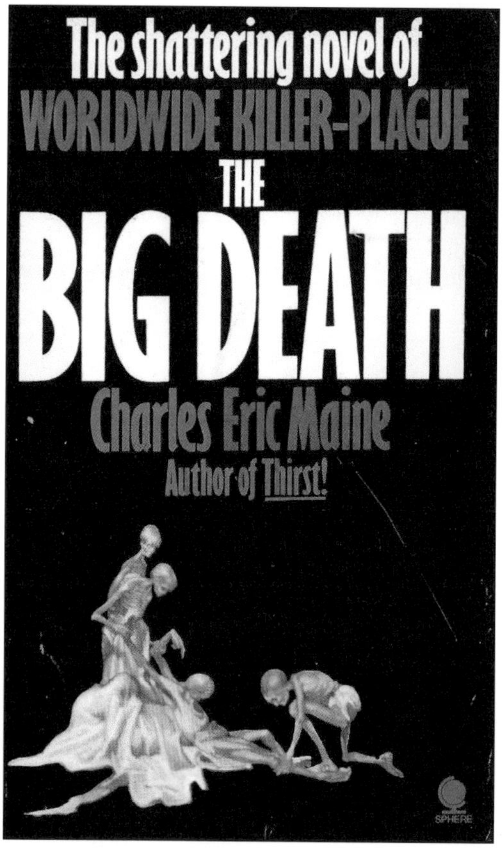
The shattering novel of
WORLDWIDE KILLER-PLAGUE
THE BIG DEATH
Charles Eric Maine
Author of Thirst!
SPHERE

FAWCETT GOLD MEDAL
Alistair MacLean
$ 250
The Satan Bug
by the author of
GOODBYE CALIFORNIA

Undersea invaders get a dose of the bubonic plague up their gills courtesy of hardman-scientist Dr Palfrey

Hector Garrido painting for a typical Baroness entry, with plenty of phallic imagery if you weren't picking up on it.

the desire. In **Tsimmis In Tangier** (1968) a chemical DRECK does the opposite, creating nymphomania to the point of utter exhaustion and death. Cut from the same flimsy cloth was **The Ring-A-Ding UFOs** (1967), the third of **The Miss From S.I.S.** series, in which iconic author 'Big' Bob Tralins' scatter-gunned any number of spy-clichés as heroine Lee Crosley investigates a town taken over by mad Chinese scientists with a phial of bubonic plague.

The most unusual employment of the bubonic plague that I read about was in the pages of **The Depths** (1967) a Dr Palfrey novel by John Creasey, whereby the hero uses the disease to wipe out a race of hostile undersea dwellers who have never encountered the disease. Shades of **War of the Worlds**, but unusual for a hero to employ such a brutal weapon. Dr Palfrey and his Department Z featured in a series of novels by the exceptionally prolific Creasey, which increasingly mixed disasters and plagues with borderline SF/espionage.

An edgier version of the sexy-spy series was **The Baroness** by Paul Kenyon (Donald Moffitt) who must sabotage **Operation Doomsday** (1974) by preventing the Russians opening a lunar capsule which contains a 'Moonstone Virus' which will kill everything living thing on Earth within 50 days. Baroness Penelope St John-Orsini does her best to sleep with every living thing on Earth within 218 pages, as anyone whose read any of the 8-book series will testify.

Moving to a more serious treatment of the theme, **Vector** (1972) details the accidental contamination of a small Utah mountain town from a nearby biological warfare installation. Author Henry Sutton (David Slavitt) focuses less on the lurid thriller elements and more on the actions of the authorities who are determined to contain the virus, and news of its leak.

The Enemy (1977) is a typically top-notch paranoid thriller from the always reliable Desmond Bagley, featuring an undercover intelligence operative who has inadvertently married into the wrong family, as his father-in-law is a defected Soviet bacteriologist. Its downbeat ending takes place at a secret germ warfare lab in Scotland, with a nasty surprise for the first-person narrator.

One of Alistair Maclean's most famous novels is **The Satan Bug** (1962) which he produced under his Ian Stuart by-line before he became the don of two-fisted thrillers following the film version of **Guns from Navarone**. The indestructible virus of the title is stolen from a secure facility, swiftly followed up by the threat by an unhinged environmentalist to release it unless the lab that produced it is destroyed. The 60th book in the long-running Nick Carter series, **The Death Strain** (1971) by Jon Messman uses the same plot-device, but what it lacks in originality it makes up for in ambition by expanding the threat to the entire world.

Mark Schorr is an author of which I know little, but his **Over Kill** (1988) is a complex and believable thriller in which a billionaire industrialist has developed a deadly virus. Lead character Robert Stark is an ex-CIA agent, and Schorr writes convincingly of this world, as well as introducing a streak of humour unusual for this dour genre.

The Doomsday Carrier (1976) opens with a chimpanzee escaping from captivity, which rather than a zoo is a government lab where it has been injected with a deadly virus that kills after 21 days. Rock-steady author Victor Canning delivers yet another archetypally British thriller, compact and relentless, well-researched and free of unnecessary operatics. That same year **Apeland** (1976) by Paul Allen was published, about a hunt for an escaped gorilla, so I imagine there must have been a news story along these lines.

Other hairy escapees include Richard Adam's **The Plague Dogs** (1977), in which two medical experiment dogs escape from a research lab and go on the run, with no-one sure whether they are carrying an infectious disease. It is very much a

Convincing spy fiction from Mark Schorr set in the shady world of CIA operatives. Cover by Al Chinchar.

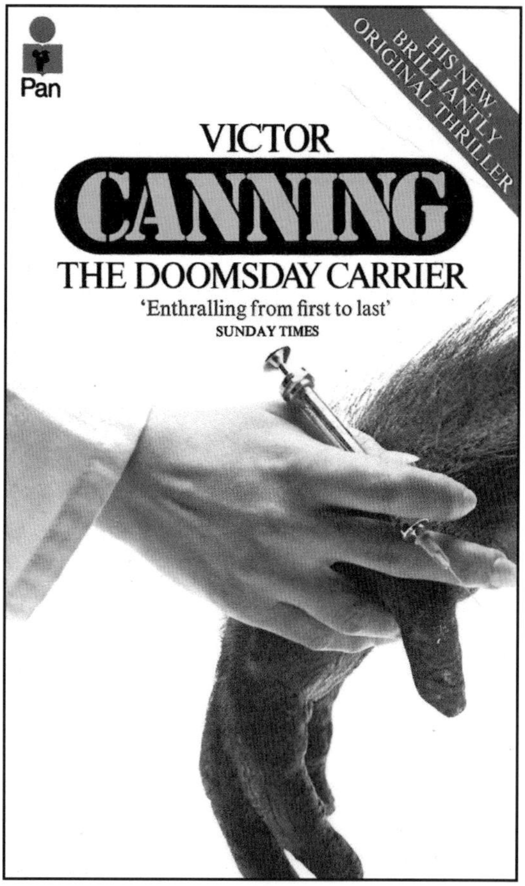

1978 UK Pan edition of Victor Canning's gripping account of an infected chimpanzee let loose in Britain.

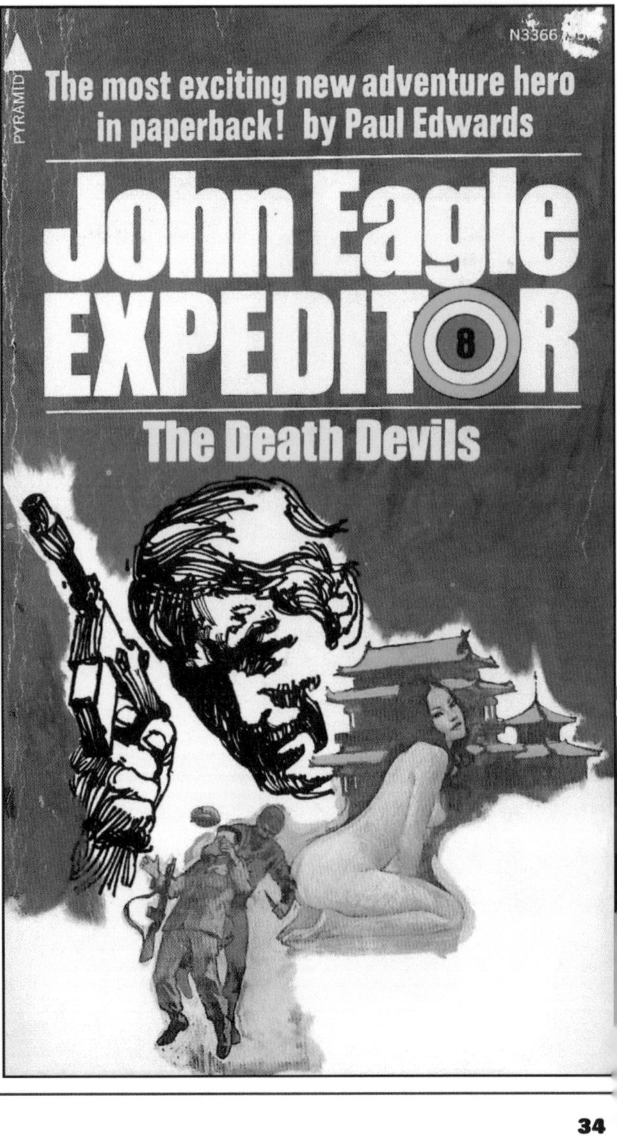

Top row - the indefatigable Nick Carter tackles any number of Commie influenzas. The Coxeman crams in more innuendoes than any other sexy-spy series.

Above - The Enforcer moved from Lancer Books to Manor to battle crop-devouring and disease carrying insects.

Right - more hungry insects on the loose, with John Eagle's finger on the RAID aerosol.

parable against vivisection, rather than a full-blooded virus-thriller.

An off shoot of the genre were those books in which the virus was used to bring the world to its knees through famine. In **Assignment Amazon Queen** (1974) the 37th in the Sam Durrell series, the indefatigable hero juggles Russian and Chinese agents deep in the Brazilian rainforests as they compete to obtain a biological weapon which renders all plant-life infertile. In Nick Carter yarn **Operation Starvation** (1966) by Nicolas Browne, a yellow peril arch-villain has developed a virus that destroys rice-crops. **Deadly Seeds** (1975) the 21st in **The Destroyer** series features the normal satire, with an eccentric millionaire claiming to have the solution for world famine with a rapid-grow Wondergrain. Of course, it's nothing of the sort.

Assault on Aimata (1975), the second in the **Cabot Cain** series by the under-rated Alan Caillou, has a criminal mastermind unleashing a plague of insects on the world to destroy all food crops. Another distant relative is **The Death Devils** (1974) the eighth in the **John Eagle** series by Paul Edwards, where Eagle is tasked with preventing the Chinese from unleashing an insect which could destroy America's agriculture. **Bio Blitz** (1975) in **The Enforcer** series had a similar theme, although the insects carried disease as well as the threat of a voracious appetite.

The vegetation could also be deadly, such as in **The Living Death** (1969) by Jon Messmann – another Nick Carter spy pot-boiler- where the world's leading scientists are being assassinated by an injection of fungus administered by a rogue agent with a grudge. In the 31st entry to **The Coxeman** series, **The Cockeyed Cuties** (1972), a gloriously un-PC book that reflects the times, the randy secret agent Rod Damon is sent in pursuit of a missing scientist who holds the key to curing a famine-creating fungus.

In the horror canon there was **Fungus** (1985, aka **Deathspore**) a gloriously bad-taste romp by Harry Adam Knight (John Brosnan and Larry Kettle) through a United Kingdom overtaken by mushrooms which sprout everywhere. **Spore-7** (1979) by Clancy Carlile has an outer-space fungus infect a Californian town, turning them into slimy, fungoid maniacs and has the president's finger hovering over the nuclear button. Shades of SF-horror film **The Quatermass Xperiment** (1955), but more likely Stephen King's **The Stand** (1978) was in the publishers' and authors' minds.

Brian Hodge wrote a version of King's bestseller, in the form of **Dark Advent** (1988) packaged as a kids-in-peril horror title. It was

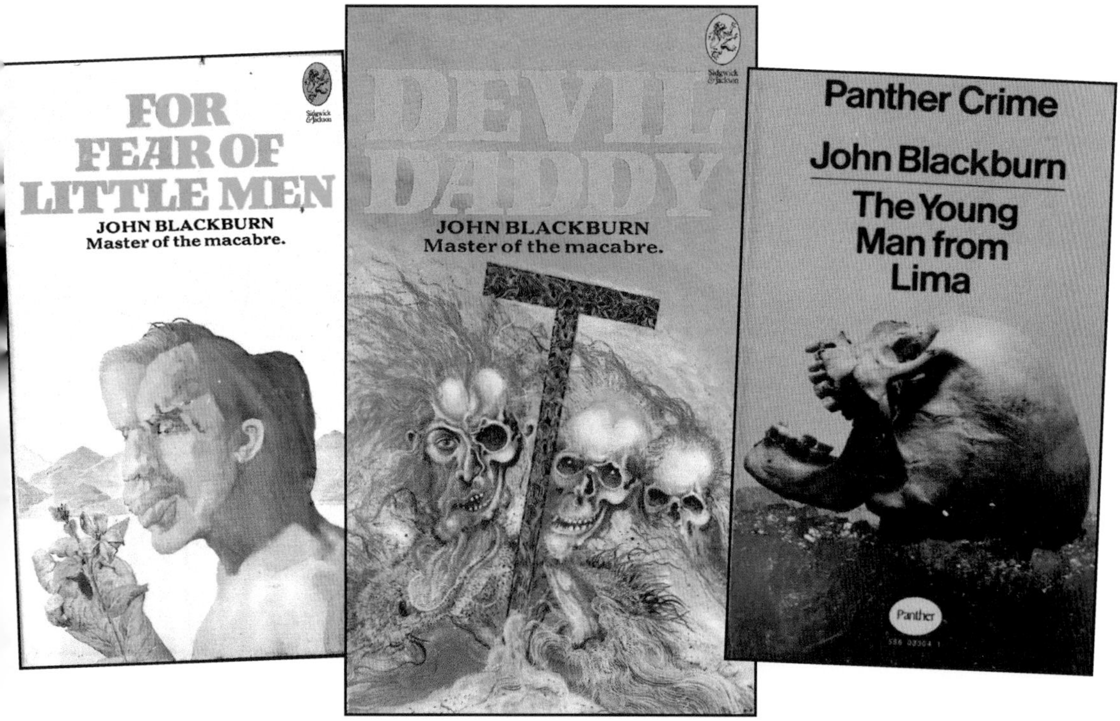

A trio from the genre-melding and consistently excellent John Blackburn. Left cover by Josh Kirby and middle by Ian Miller.

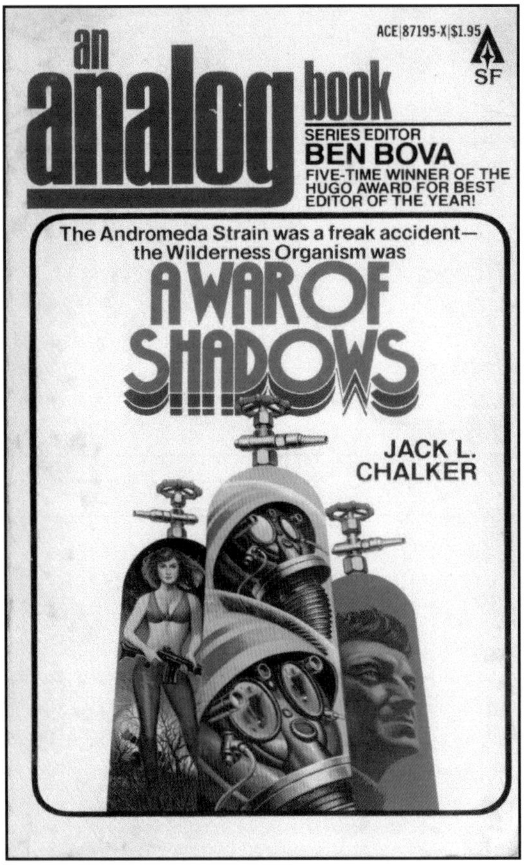

Left - Chalker's near-future thriller was part of a series of books issued by Ace in association with SF mag Analog.
Right - Although the identity of John Lange as Michael Crichton is not mentioned on the cover, it is on the spine
Opposite - George Wilson cover for a UK reprint of Conaway's horror-thriller which was derivative of The Fog

nothing of the sort, played out in a cast of good versus evil in a world destroyed by a weaponised plague.

Pick of the crop was **A Scent of New-Mown Hay** (1958), the first published work of John Blackburn, an author of the finest pedigree whose genre-meshing works carry a guarantee of a top-notch read. Starting off as a Cold War thriller it soon evolves into something far more chilling as a mutant fungus developed by a Nazi scientist escapes and exacts a terrible toll.

Blackburn would consistently employ viruses and plagues in his fiction; **Young Man from Lima** (1968) concerns a parasite which, when injected into the human bloodstream, brings on a state of euphoria, enhanced physical powers and thinking. As long as a lichen-based supplement is consumed – stop that and an agonising death follows. **Devil Daddy** (1972) unfolds the secrets surrounding a virus that instantly ages its victims, moving from a whodunnit to out and out goose-bumper – a personal favourite.

Running it close was **For Fear of Little Men** (1972) which was an archetypally Blackburn combination of supernatural legends with a local flavour, Nazi war-criminals hiding out whilst cooking up dastardly plans, and an unexplained outbreak of a virus. British cult author Guy N Smith was Blackburn's nearest rival in terms of how often viruses appeared in his many eco-horrors, and I'll look at him shortly.

The Time of the Fourth Horseman (1979) was set in a near future where vaccination has eradicated disease, when a renegade cell of the CIA decide to replace a vaccine with a placebo which leads to a deadly outbreak of previously eradicated diseases. Perhaps not material one would associate Chelsea Quinn Yarbro, who is most well-known for her St Germain vampire series, but a suitably pacey

THE DEADLY SPRING
A DEADLY CHEMICAL RELEASED THE SAVAGE NATURE OF EVERYONE IN TOWN.
J.C. CONAWAY

Above- GAAAAS! Sex and rage inducing gases a-go-go! Outdated spy romp Ban the Bra was the fifth in the Gerry Ransom series. The Fog was James Herbert's tour-de-force of a "hob-nail boots on a lacquered table" horror-thriller. 3,000 copies of The Gas were seized at one point by Manchester police in 1980! Cover by Harry Douthwaite.

story with an open-ending, and a thought-provoking message.

Another near-future scenario was played out in **War of Shadows** (1979) opening with a series of strange and terrible diseases striking America's small towns. This was soon discarded for a more action-focussed plot about terrorists, from SF-author Jack Chalker. Along similar lines was **Wellspring** (1978), by Edward Hawkins, where the Colorado River is poisoned by a terrorist who commits suicide and leaves time-bombs of the virus which will contaminate America's favourite drinking water.

Binary (1972) was the eighth book by Michael Crichton to appear under his John Lange by-line, in which a secret agent is tasked with preventing a right-wing businessman from killing the president and thousands of bystanders on a street parade with poison gas. It is a familiar plot, but Critchon makes it credible enough and provides a gripping cat and mouse thriller.

The Last Canadian (1974) is a survivalist novel, in which the resourceful lead senses that the plague that has begun to spread will prove devastating, so whisks his family off to a remote log cabin in the Rockies. William Heine debut novel is a fine post-apocalyptic tale and reflects the Cold War concerns that were intensifying at that time.

Insanity, often leading to extreme violence or sexuality, caused by a virus was a popular theme. In **The Midnight Dancers** (1971), a rare excursion into fiction by comics author Gerry Conway, mankind is wiped out by a space plague that causes insanity. **The Deadly Spring** (1976) by sound-a-like J C Conaway has an earthquake hitting a military base, resulting in a chemical leaking into the drinking water for townspeople who are then removed of their inhibitions. I imagine that author Conaway was given a copy of James Herbert's **The Fog** to replicate, as his book also contains homicidal school-children, death by garden-shears and strong sexual content. Unfortunately it is missing all the other elements that make **The Fog** such a ferocious read.

In **Killer's Cargo** (1974), the twelfth adventure of The Butcher, he is competing with rival agents to obtain a deadly gas that instantly drives the inhaler into a rabid killing fit. One of the more bizarre thrillers in this category was **The Minotaur Factor** (1976) by Stuart Stern, in which the contraceptive pill triggers homicidal rages, with the opening chapter's swinging party interrupted by one young debutante going wild with a ceremonial sword. Stern was a pen-name for Hugh C Rae, which he also used for **The Poison Tree** (1978), which I haven't a copy, but also looks like a killer-virus title.

Distant relatives to **The Minotaur Factor** include **Blue Sunshine** (1977) by Ken Johnson, a tie-in to a B-movie about a rogue dose of LSD which causes its users to lose their hair and acquire murderous impulses, and **Gloryhits** (1978) by Bob Stickgold and Mark Noble where couples taking acid whilst trying for babies find their new-born just a little bit different. There was the truly bizarre **The Styx Complex** (1977) by Russell Rhodes, in which a megalomaniac beautician who treats the world's most famous population starts killing them off with brain implants and replacing them with doppelgangers. File under "Plots rejected for The Baroness as too ludicrous".

For sex inducing gases, see **The Gas** (1970) by Charles Platt and **Ban the Bra** (1968) by Jay Martin, which are extreme opposites in terms of sexual frankness and politics. Platt's notorious account of the transformation of Britain following the leak of an aphrodisiac gas, was apparently written as an intentionally offensive book, either as a hostile response to the world or as an attempt to cast off British repressions before the author moved to America. Martin's throw-a-way story of hippy scientists Slick and Brick inventing a sex gas, is part of a **Gerry Ransom** series, very much in the tradition of the pun-filled and zany **Man from ORGY** sexy-spy genre. There was also a movie tie-in to black comedy **Gas! or It Became Necessary to Destroy the World in Order to Save It** (1970), concerning a lethal gas leak that kills everyone over age 25.

Back to men's adventure, **The Penetrator 25: Floating Death** (1978) has a renegade scientist who wishes to bring American to its knees through a series of plagues, whether killing off its cattle with bubonic plague or releasing virus-filled balloons. Mark Roberts was behind the Lionel Derrick house name for this shabby episode. The Penetrator's 53rd and final mission, was a visit to **City Of The Dead** (1984) to prevent the KGB going into production at a biological warfare plant in Bolivia.

Bob Stickgold seemed vexed by the sexual revolution, with his only two novels about birth control and the war of the sexes. Cover by Richard Newton.

The Minotaur Factor was another take on the contraceptive pill, with the opening scene reminiscent of John Farris' classic but baffling All Heads Turn When the Hunt Rides by.

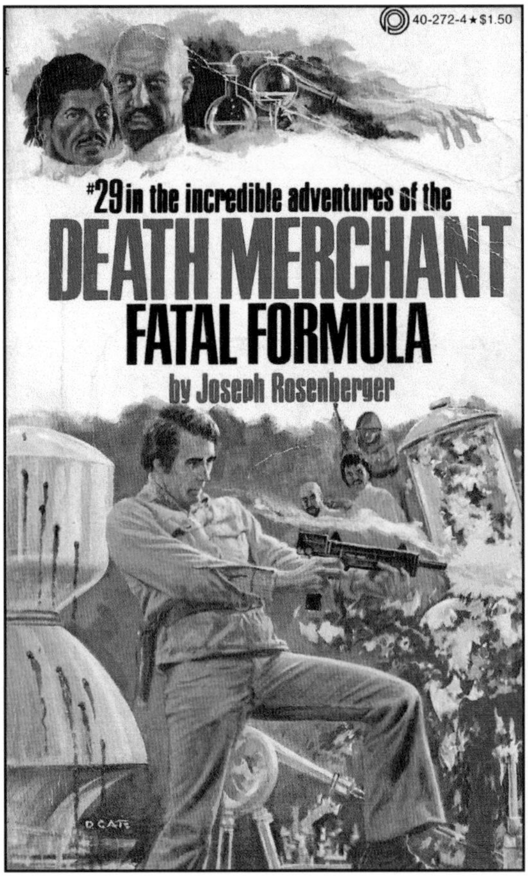

In **Death Merchant 5: Satan Strike** (1973), the sadistic dictator of a Caribbean island develops a deadly virus which he plans to use to trigger WW3. There follows an uneasy alliance between Russia and America as they send their top agents to defeat the plan. In **Death Merchant 13: The Mato Grosso Horror** (1978), the Israeli Secret Service request the CIA's assistance to eradicate a group of ex-Nazis holed up in the Brazilian rain-forest who are producing biological weapons. In **Death Merchant 29 Fatal Formula** (1978) there is a secret plot by the KGB to develop a super-flu. Death Merchant creator Joseph Rosenberger has a unique writing style and take on life (and death). Everyone should read one Joseph Rosenberger book in their life – no more than one, no less.

Staying in the men's adventure canon, the **Butler** series had two encounters with viruses; **Chinese Roulette** (Leonard Levinson, 1979) started with vials of bubonic plague smuggled through Hong Kong and **Killer Virus** (author unknown, 1983) commences with the mystery as to how Butler's arch-enemies Hydra have massacred a religious cult without any apparent weaponry.

The Deadly Prey (1975) was the fourth of **The Hunter** series by the dependable Ralph Hayes, with hero John Yard commissioned to track down a twisted scientist in Appalachia who is developing the Beta Variation, a virus deadlier than the bubonic plague which he has been testing on unwitting locals. In **The Judas Soldiers** (1987) by Frank Garrett, the fourth of the ten-book **Dirty Dozen** style men's adventure series **Kill Squad**, a splinter group of disenchanted CIA operatives obtain a large quantity of a highly dangerous virus which they plan to unleash on their own country.

In the ninth Matt Helm novel, **The Devastators** (1965), Helm hot-foots to London and then Scotland in order to stop a mad scientist who plans to unleash a new Black Plague upon the world. The thirteenth Helm novel, **The Poisoners** (1971) was concerned with a plot to spread pollution.

By dint of having more adventures than any other men's adventure character, Nick Carter had many, many close encounters with deadly viruses.

and germs. **The Bright Blue Death** (1967) by Nicolas Browne has a Fourth Reich developing a new disease. **The Arab Plague** (1970) by Jon Messmann a reference to mind-controlling drugs used on world leaders. **The Death Strain** (1970) by Jon Messmann has an activist group whose hippy-image belies their intent to unleash a lethal virus which brings an excruciating death to its victims.

The Omega Terror (1972) is the pet-project of Dr Zano a rogue microbiologist whose whole being is consumed with hatred for the US and developing a virus to destroy it. **The Doomsday Spore** (1979) by George Warren has a flesh-eating spore from outer space unleashed by a terrorist group. Carter has to unlock **The Strontium Code** (1981) by David Hagberg, when he retrieves a deadly canister from a Japanese tanker.

Operation McMurdo Sound (1982), also by David Hagberg, has Carter visiting a virus research centre in Antarctica where all contact has suddenly been lost. In another Carter, **Doctor DNA** (1982) by Robert E. Vardeman, the super-villain Dr. Faber has a plan to kill thousands with highly infectious tsetse flies. Non-Carter book, **The St Francis Effect** (1976), also presents death on wings, in the form of mosquitoes spreading a new and deadly virus, with author Zach Hughes pitching at the medical-thriller market.

Sam Durrell, the long-running secret agent series that ran out of steam a long time before it was cancelled, oft stumbled over viruses. Best was **Assignment Tokyo** (1971) – despite being a later entry – in which a canister that washes up on the shores of a Japanese fishing village wipes out all bar one beautiful girl. **Assignment Death Ship** (1983), the 48th and final entry in the series, has Durrell investigating a ship-wreck where the passengers all died from a mysterious illness.

Another series which outstayed its welcome was the **K'ing Kung Fu** run of seven chop-socky pulps at Freeway Press, although it has something of a cult following due to its wild fight scenes and

Two of the finest men's adventure paperback covers of all time. Above - Bob Larkin paints the Kill Squad. Left - Ken Barr brings The Hunter to life.

Serious-minded thriller which imagined the impact of bats with anthrax escaping from a military laboratory.

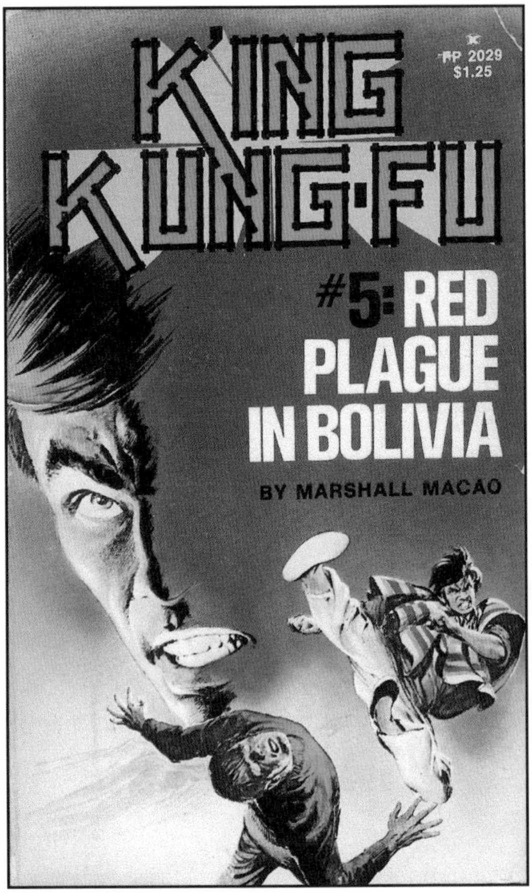

Comics industry veteran Dick Giordano's image was reminiscent of style of the famous comics artist Neal Adams

castrated arch-villain Kak Nan Tang. **Red Plague in Bolivia** (1974) was a lesser entry to the series which is one-note at best, with Kak setting up a germ factory in South America.

In **Huntsville Horror** (1991), the ninth in the **Overload** series, part of the short-lived trucker craze, a pair of ex-Special Forces operatives turned "rig-jockeys" are tasked with delivering satellite parts to a military lab, which is taken over by terrorists to get their hands on the viral weapons being developed there.

Viruses and plagues were a popular device with horror writers, whether it be rabies -as well as King's **Cujo**, there were many examples of rabid Euro-poodles in UK paperbacks - or AIDs – which resulted in a horde of vampire novels. British author Guy N Smith was a super-spreader of pulp viruses, starting with **Bats from Hell** (1978) in which the titular creatures are inadvertently set free when a love-rat of a scientist has a violent argument with his ex-lover in their laboratory. The furry flyers carry a deadly strain of meningitis, and various authority figures from Smith's youth die horribly.

Bats had also been used in **Project Dracula** (1971) by Alan Scott (reprinted as **The Anthrax Mutation** by Pyramid US), where they have been weaponised as carriers of Anthrax in the confines of secret military laboratory until a mysterious explosion sets them loose in the United Kingdom. This is a seriously minded novel, based on research and focused on the worldwide socio-political impact of such an instance.

Guy Smith also delivered **Thirst** (1980) in which a lorryload of deadly weed-killer crashes into the water reservoir that supplies Birmingham, resulting in riots, anarchy and infected lunatics. Another one of Smith's womanising-scientist-bearded-hero types saves the day. That is until **Thirst 2: The Plague** (1987) when the disease returns to the remote village where the lorry originally crashed, just as it become cut-off due to heavy snow-fall. One of Smith's more intense works, less in the

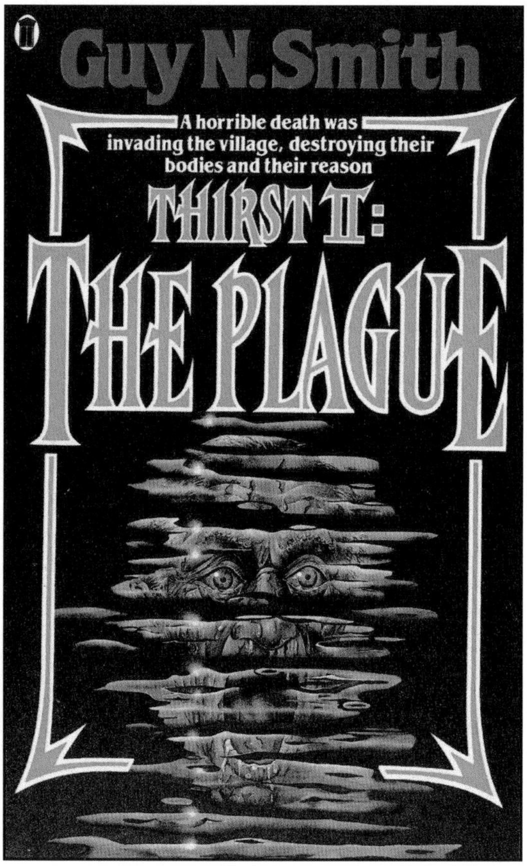

This horror-thriller follow-up to The Thirst only received the solitary printing in English language.

A rare hardback outing for Guy Smith, which unfortunately lacks his customary bite.

horror genre, but certainly laced with the bizarre sex and gloopy gore his fans expect.

Poisoned water is the origin of Smith's **The Festering** (1989) after a traveller suffering with hideous lesions is hung by the local witch-finder and buried deep beneath the village, which centuries later is bored into for a well. You can probably work out from the title what happens to anyone infected. **The Plague Chronicles** (1993) was a lacklustre effort from Smith before he retired from fiction, reliant on biblical plagues and recycling Smith's previous books, as a world-wide drought drives a bickering family to escape to the country.

Arguably writing in the vein of Smith and selling in large numbers in the UK was Mark Ronson (Mark Alexander), an ex-journalist earning some coin with a side-line in horror books, who dug up **Plague Pit** (1982). A no-nonsense nasty in which an incompetent and drunk builder inadvertently cracks open a medieval burial chamber in which plague victims were buried and makes off with their gold jewellery and a few extra microscopic guests. It is down to a journalist to expose the deadly virus, and for Ronson to disgust readers with gallons of pus leaking from lesions. Yum.

Successfully operating in a similar arena was **Devil's Kiss** (1984), a splattery re-setting of **The Fog**, where sewer-workers inadvertently open a phial of flesh-eating virus, which also induces psychotic rages. A slim yet decent effort from John Hyde, which delivers on everything you might desire from such a book.

Gary Brander unleashed **The Brain Eaters** (1985), with a title reminiscent of a 50s Red Scare SF movie, but a no-frills and gory pot-boiler which is fun and fast-paced. The titular organism literally devours its victims' brains from the inside which causes violent outbursts. In a similar vein was John Russo's **Inhuman** (1986), where terrorists surviving an air-crash revert to a lizard-brain state and rampage through a couple's retreat.

Rabid (1977) was a tie-in to the David

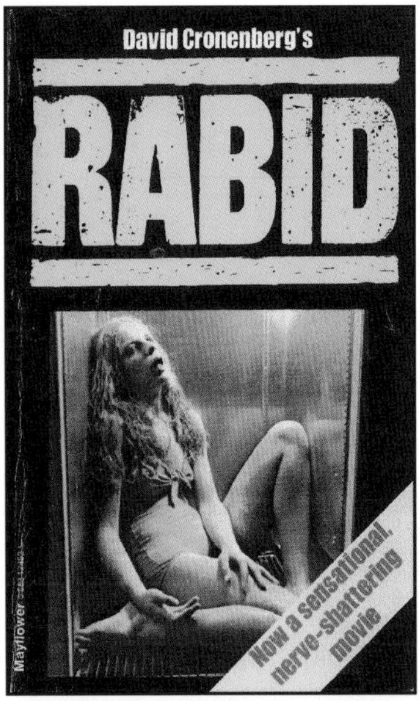

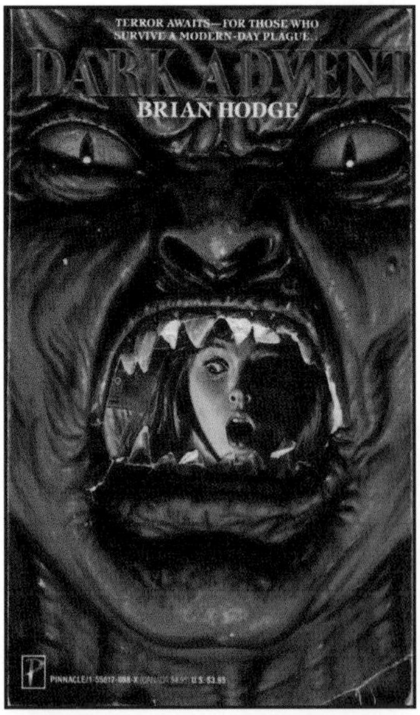

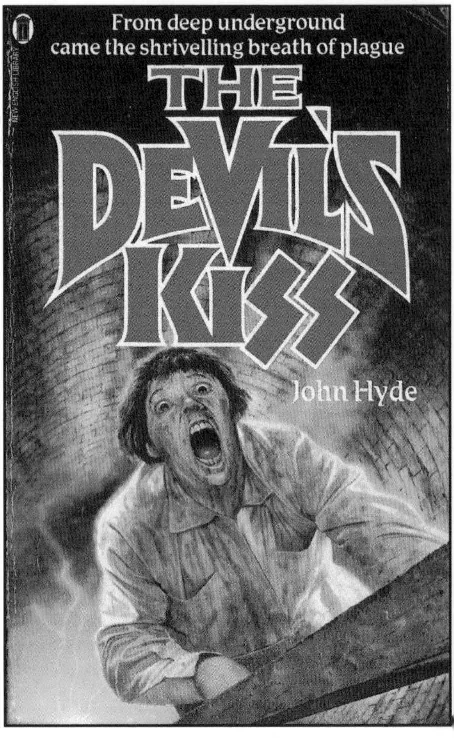

Dark Advent - Bob Larkin provided the brilliant but misleading cover and frontispiece for Brian Hodge's debut novel Dark Advent.

This US edition of Plague Pit appeared six years after its only UK printing.

The Devil's Kiss carried an uncredited cover that wa possibly by Les Edwards.

Opposite - one of two UK tie-ins to The Incredible Melting Man, with this one painted by Joe Petagno.

manages to up the sleaze and quease of Cronenberg's typically disturbing original.

For the most part it strikes me that SF focused on dealing with the aftermath of a virulent plague, rather than the ordeal of fighting it, using it to wipe clean the Earth apart from a handful of chosen survivors who then face the challenge of rebuilding. **The Purple Cloud** (1901) by M P Shiel was an early example, in which the titular object devastates the population, leaving a man and woman with the responsibility of starting again. **Earth Abides** (1949) by George Stewart was a more sophisticated exploration of the theme, as was **False Night** (1954 aka **Some Will Not Die**) by Algis Budrys.

The race-to-space of the 60s did inspire some "what ifs" as to returning astronauts bringing back outer-space sniffles. **The Andromeda Strain** (1969) by Michael Critchon was a bestselling account of a returning satellite contaminated by a virus which consumes a town and a remote nuclear facility. Its appetite to consume material such as plastic and metal may have in some way inspired Kit Pedler and Gerry Davis' **Mutant 59: The Plastic Eater** (1972) which could have easily sat in the disaster article in this issue, as it devours airplanes and underground trains with dire results for the passengers.

The Incredible Melting Man (1978) was Phil Smith's tie-in to the 1977 film which has become something of a cult classic due to its schizophrenic and gory take on **The Quatermass Xperiment**. An astronaut returns to earth unaware that he has contracted a space-virus which melts his skin and gives him a cannibalistic appetite. A more benign relative was an element in **The Apollo Legacy** (1970) in which an illicit affair between a noted Apollo astronaut and a female journalist results in a pregnancy which might be in trouble due to a space virus. I have not read Harry Harrison's **Plague from Space** (1965), but I believe the title to be literal and in keeping with the theme of this piece.

Whilst writing this article in June 2020, the internet carried stories of how the e-book version of **Eyes of Darkness** (1981) by Dean Koontz (as Leigh Nichols) had hit the top of the bestseller charts due to its storyline apparently predicting COVID-19's origins. Based on this commercial success, I imagine the tradition of the virus-thriller will be continuing for many years to come.

JUSTIN MARRIOTT goes behind the bars to investigate the authors in lockdown that produced fiction whilst under lock and key.

PROSE AND CONS

E Howard Hunt (1918 - 2007) is probably the most infamous of convicted felons who doubled as an author, serving 33 months in prison during the mid-70s for his role in bugging the Democrats in the Watergate scandal on behalf of Richard Nixon. His Wikipedia page reads like the ultimate conspiracy-thriller, with Hunt pulling any number of other stunts to advance Nixon's position, as well as adding his name to the list of suspects in the assassination of JFK. Previously to working directly for Nixon, Hunt had spent four decades in the CIA, where he also found the time to produce a solid body of fiction through the 50s and 60s. His pseudonyms included David St John for a series of occult thrillers, Gordon Davis for hardboiled 'tec fiction at Gold Meal, and Robert Dietrich, most notably for a series of Steve Bentley stories. During the 1970s, reprinted editions by Signet and Pinnacle of his pre-Watergate books proudly trumpeted his Watergate credentials.

Chester Himes (1909-1984) is one of the greatest crime authors of all time, with his **Coffin Ed and Gravedigger Jones** series still being reprinted half-a-century on. Himes began writing whilst serving a lengthy jail sentence for attempted bank robbery. By all accounts Himes criminal activities were a by-product from the traumatic experience as a teenager of seeing his brother, who had been blinded during an accident, refused treatment by white doctors in hospital because he was African-American. Bored with prison life, Himes began writing short pieces, sometimes using his prison number 59623 as a by-line, which were published in magazines such as **Esquire**. Released early for good behaviour, Himes expanded into writing novels, such as **If He Hollers Let Him Go**, **Cotton Comes to Harlem** and **The Real Cool Killers**. Dissatisfied with the continued inequality he experienced in America, such as being kicked off the Warner Bros lot by a prejudiced exec, Himes moved to Europe in the mid-1950s where he lived until his death.

Robert Beck (1918- 1992) is better recognised under his pimp name of Iceberg Slim, which he adopted for a series of hard-hitting memoirs-meet-fiction books, starting with **Pimp** (1967). According to accounts, Beck had served a prison term in 1961, and upon release decided he could no longer cut it as a pimp, but a memoir of that life could make him money. The resulting book was an unflinching and uncompromising story of that life, and when nascent sleaze publisher Holloway House published it, it sold hundreds of thousands of copies. Beck followed it up with **Trick Baby**, which was made into a successful low-budget movie, and his best

SIGNET • 451-Q5779 • 95c
CONVICTED WATERGATE CONSPIRATOR
E. HOWARD HUNT
former CIA agent writing as David St. John
Return from Vorkuta
CIA's agent-in-disguise, PETER WARD, gets caught in a shadowy espionage world of murder and intrigue.

#6
SIGNET-451-Y6805-$1.25
CHESTER HIMES
HOT DAY, HOT NIGHT
(formerly titled: Blind Man with a Pistol)
Coffin Ed and Grave Digger Jones face murder and madness when Harlem erupts in a riot of wild sex and bloody violence....
"The best writer of mayhem yarns since Raymond Chandler!"
—San Francisco Chronicle

PIMP
the story of my life
by ICEBERG SLIM
HH-139
ADULT READING

BH464 $150
Drugs, murder and a greedy pimp hang up a black hit man!
DONALD GOINES
DADDY COOL
THE GREATEST GHETTO WRITER THAT EVER LIVED!

Mink by John Springs III, was written in 1985, supposedly due to a bet made whilst he was in jail.

Bottom - God's Renegade was a first person memoir of a biker, part of the short-lived Scorpio imprint.

in my opinion, **The Long White Con**. Holloway House went onto commercial success by specialising in fiction aimed at African-Americans, and Beck's family sued them when he died penniless despite selling millions of books.

A career criminal as a means to feed his voracious drug addiction, Donald Goines (1936-1974) was serving one of his many prison terms when he read Iceberg Slim's **Pimp** in a Michigan prison, and switched his efforts from westerns to gritty urban noir. Holloway House were his outlet, and Goines served them product at a rapid rate, supposedly to fund his addiction without returning to crime. 11 books under his own name were published by Holloway House, most famously **Dopefiend** and **Street Players**, as well as 5 books as Al Clark including 4 in the **Kenyatta** series. Goines died in an unsolved murder case, speculated to be related to drug debts or gangsters unhappy at the thinly-veiled versions of them in his books.

A lesser known convict author published at Holloway House was John Springs III. Imprisoned for armed robbery during the 80s and 90s, he wrote five books for Holloway House including **Kansas**, **Mink** and **The Pocket**. Apparently, he wrote his first book based on a bet with three other inmates, with **Kansas** the result. I suspect it was the people he dedicated the book to, including Sweet Daddy Dimp, for "lending me his raggedy typewriter".

An unusual attempt to replicate the Holloway House was rolled out by Zebra Books, who as a newer paperback house were always eager to experiment in search of market share. Under the editorial direction of Frank Earl Andrews they launched Scorpio Books, a short-lived imprint showcasing "the best in prison break out talent." Andrews had previously published fiction produced by felons, having edited three anthologies for Pyramid: **Voices from the Big House**, **Over the Wall** and **Prose and Cons** early in the 1970s.

The Scorpio books mainly fell into the prison memoir category, with **God's Renegade** by John North, **Dig the ***** let's Kill Him Again** by Robert E Chinn and **Prison Diary** by Edward Conway. There was one work of fiction in the form of **Underground** by John Dutton about a super-max and brutal subterranean prison, an excursion into **One Flew Over the Cuckoo's Nest** territory in **The Day They Scrambled My Brains at the Funny Factory** by Max Rabinowitz, and two memoirs in the style of **Pimp**

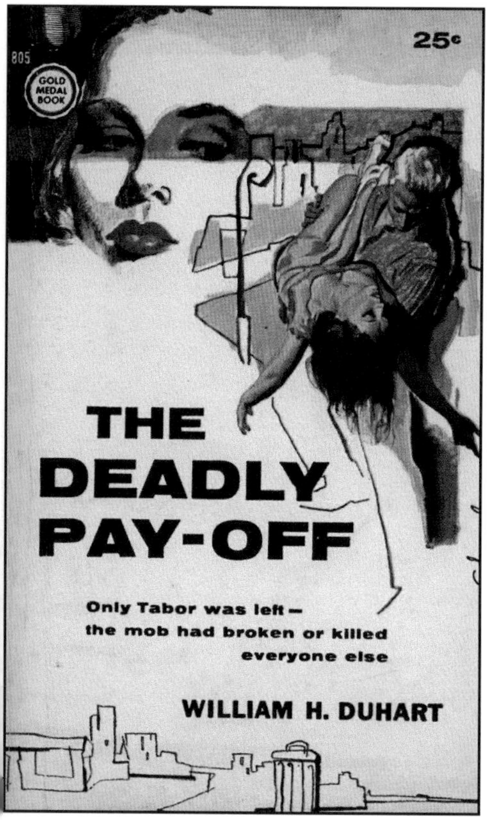

Felony Tank was Braly's first novel, semi-biographical and written in jail under the guidance of Gold medal editor Knox Burger.

Bottom - The Deadly Pay-Off was one of William Duhart's few commercially successful writing efforts.

with **Black Prince** by Anonymous and **The Virginia Ratt** by Ratton Hall and Sandy Sidar.

Another publisher with a link to convicts aspiring to be authors was the legendary Gold Medal. Knox Burger (1922-2010), the equally legendary editor, apparently mentored at least one inmate. Malcolm Braly (1925 – 1980) spent almost half of his life doing hard time in places like Folsom, San Quentin, and Nevada State prison. However, he was a more talented writer than criminal, and whilst serving time, had three paperbacks published by the celebrated Gold Medal - **Felony Tank**, **Shake Him Till He Rattles**, and **It's Cold Out There**. Apparently, Braly's most celebrated work **On the Yard**, written while on parole, had been subject to suppression by the prison authorities; concerned about the negative P.R. from such a book, the board threatened that writing it was in contravention to parole terms. Braly wrote the autobiography **False Starts** but his career as a writer was cut short by a fatal car accident.

Another Gold Medal contributor, although uncredited, was Albert Nussbaum (1934 – 1996), a fan turned writer, he just happened to be serving a forty-year prison term for bank robbery when he wrote to author Dan J Marlowe to express his admiration for how well he had captured the criminal philosophy in the hardboiled classic **The Name of the Game is Death**. There are two excellent essays in **I, Witness*** (edited by Brian Garfield) where the two outline their working relationship which sprung from that initial letter. Gold Medal mainstay Marlowe states that he left out some of Nussbaum's technical advice on safe-cracking for fear of producing how-to-manuals for bank-robbers! He also played a key role in helping Nussbaum secure parole in the early 70s, who went on to a career of short stories, novels and TV scripts.

William H Duhart (1921-2003) had a single book at Gold Medal; **The Deadly Pay-Off**. Duhart had been convicted in 1952 for 3-18 years for assault and armed robbery, when he and a female accomplice claimed to be from the gas board and stole $5000 cash from a home-owner. He was released from Wisconsin State prison in 1957 on parole for good behaviour. Apparently, he moved to a writer's commune in Illinois, where as well as the Gold Medal one-off, he produced a screenplay for an unmade movie and a flurry of short stories for sleazy

****I, Witness** contains a great essay from Lawrence Block on his brush with the law in Mexico as a young thrill-seeker.*

crime digest magazines such as **Keyhole Detective**. Presumably he was able to make more money in other trades, so the trace disappears there.

Elmer Merle Parsons (1926-?) began selling novels to Gold Medal while he was a convict in San Quentin. He had led a life of crime, convicted of burglary, car theft and passing stolen cheques, and was serving one of his terms when he sold his first novel, **Self Made Widow**, which was published under the pseudonym Philip Race. This was followed up by **Killer Take All** and **Johnny Come Deadly**, also under the Race name, until upon his release in 1960 Parsons was able to publish under his own name. He released a couple of westerns before moving into the more lucrative world of TV scripts for household name series such as **Bonanza** and **Flipper**.

Another author-criminal at Gold Medal, but who was never jailed, was Milton Ozaki (1913 - 1989), who in the 1970s, after his paperback career had faltered, ran several mail order frauds from Chicago.

Another Gold Medal connection can be found in mystery writer Anne Perry (1938-), who although never published by them, had an account of her role in an infamous murder documented as **Evil Friends,** a Gold Medal written by Vin Packer. Peter Jackson later made it into the film **Heavenly Creatures**.

Like Donald Goines, Edward Bunker (1933-2005) was inspired by a fellow convict that had been published. But rather than meeting him through a book, Bunker's neighbour whilst in solitary at San Quentin was Caryl Chessman, convicted murderer and author of the best-selling **Cell 2455, Death Row**. This inspired Bunker to begin writing, but his early manuscripts were lost or destroyed as part of his criminal lifestyle. Eventually all of these drafts became **No Beast So Fierce**, which was published just as Bunker was earning parole, a searing account of a career criminal's release from jail and his losing battle to integrate back into mainstream society. Dustin Hoffman bought the film rights, which was released as **Straight Time**, and I imagine the money was able to help Bunker make the right choices, unlike his doomed lead Max Dembo. Bunker went on to write more, notably **The Animal Factory**, before Hollywood began to draw on his experiences and talents. He experienced something of a renaissance following his role as Mr Blue in Tarantino's **Reservoir Dogs** and his books were bought back into print.

Unlike Bunker, Emil Richard Johnson (1938 – 1997) was unable to leave his criminal lifestyle behind. Johnson used his experience as an Army intelligence sergeant to

The Dark of Summer mixed crime-noir with a romantic-thriller, as a man-on-the-run encounters a number of women.

Bottom - Although it is clearly a likeness of Dustin Hoffman on the cover, the actor looked very different in the film version.

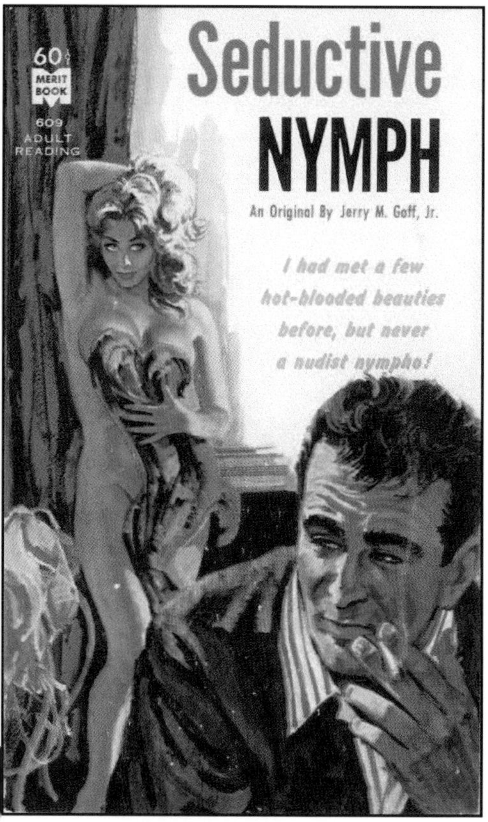

become an armed robber and was sentenced to 40 years at Minnesota's Stillwater Correctional Facility after he killed someone in a botched caper. Johnson wiled away the lockdown time by writing, and won the 1969 Best First Novel Edgar Award for his hardboiled detective procedural **Silver Street**, but had to accept the award in the prison visitors' room. Whilst still imprisoned he followed it up with the super hard-boiled **Mongo's Back in Town** (which was filmed for TV as **Steel Wreath**) and prison-riot classic **Cage Five is Going to Blow**. Johnson abandoned his writing career when he escaped prison, returning to drugs and crime, and his next stint inside was not productive in producing any more books.

There were two prisoner authors that I know of that, in addition to their convicted crimes, also stole other author's works and passed it off as their own. The most prolific plagiariser was Jerry Goff, whose name and that of his pseudonym Jerry Lane, appeared on many covers from Chicago based publisher Camerarts on their Merit imprint, typically carrying painted covers by Robert Bonfils. According to research from Lynn Munroe, Richard Prather of **Shell Scott** fame received a letter from a fan saying he had been reading a Jerry Goff novel and spotted large sections that had been lifted from Prather's works. By all accounts, Goff was serving his third term in jail when questioned about this plagiarism, and blithely confessed to doing this multiple times whilst submitting his manuscripts. Prather's lawsuit was against Camerarts, and based on it being the largest case of plagiarism seen in court at that point, he received $40k compensation. My sympathies to the light-fingered Goff, as based on rumour, the owners of Camerarts were the type of businessmen whose 'associates' may well have expected repayment from Goff.

One rip-off that struck at the heart of the English publishing industry and critics was perpetrated by Don Robson, a young English prisoner who copied word-for-word an obscure sleaze novel and submitted it as his own work in a competition aimed at encouraging art amongst prisoners. **Young and Sensitive** won and was published in hardback by Penguin Books to much acclaim. Before the paperback edition could be published, a member of the public tipped off Penguin that it was a copy of **Fires of Youth**, originally published at Magnet Books by Charles Williams. Fair play to Penguin who then published a paperback of **Fires of Youth**, credited to James Lincoln Collier who had been using Charles Williams as a pen-name. Lynn Munroe tells the fascinating story at his

Mongo's Back in Town was a super hardboiled account of a hit-man returning home to kill his brother and take his wife.

Bottom - Robert Bonfils cover painting for one of Jerry Goff's ran-sackings of Richard Prather's Shell Scott novels.

excellent web-site and makes the point that many sleaze novels were unjustly dismissed by critics because of their sensationalist packaging. Having read a few sleaze books by the likes of Block, Silverberg and Westlake, I can't say I agree with Lynn, and that Robson either had great taste or struck lucky with his source.

Two ladies make this list of usual suspects, with the second UK author Joan Henry (1914-2000). Born into a wealthy and well-connected family, Henry had been an early 20th century author of romance novels until sentenced to a year in prison in 1951 when she attempted to pass a fraudulent cheque. Shocked at the harsh treatment she observed of fellow prisoners, Henry turned her outrage into the autobiographical **Who Lie in Gaol**, which became a bestseller and the basis for 1954 film **The Weak and the Wicked**. Her next novel **Yield to the Night**, carried a strong anti-capital punishment message which became a real-life talking point in the UK as it was published as Ruth Ellis became the last woman to be hanged in Britain.

Frank Elli (1925 – 1984) only had one published novel, but it won the $10,000 Thomas R. Coward award from publishers Coward-McCann in 1966 and was made into a successful film. **The Riot** was drawn from Eli's experiences serving eleven jail terms, most specifically as an inmate during the Walla Walla prison riots where he had been serving a burglary sentence. At the time it was acknowledged as the most authentic prison novel yet written, with a gripping "you are there" style. I'm reading it at the moment, and it's so good at dragging you into the world of the inmate and the titular riot, I am staggered that Elli didn't complete any further books.

Another convict whose output was limited was Thomas D Carroll, whose literary career consisted of two crime potboilers published at Lancer in the 1968. **Grounds for Murder** was a revenge themed debut, with packaging highlighting Carroll being on Death Row. The book was terrible, perhaps only noteworthy to paperback historians due to the involvement of Michael Avallone who was thanked in the dedication. Avallone's role is not clear, although it is understood that he did not ghost-write it.

Well educated and a decorated WW2 veteran, Russell Trainer (1921 –1992) nonetheless chose to make a living as a con-man, which ended in 1959 when he was sent to a Michigan jail for passing a dud cheque. Whilst in jail, Trainer penned **The Warden's Wife**, an account of the frisky lady of the title who was the object of unbridled lust

1953 paperback edition from Doubleday of Joan Henry's critique of the British penal system.

Bottom - UK Pan movie tie-in to The Riot, which was Frank Elli's only novel, despite being a critical and commercial success.

from frustrated convicts. It was published by sleaze house Beacon Books, and Trainer went onto a long career in that genre of paperbacks, even establishing his own imprint. Several of his sleaze titles carried a prison theme, including **Denied, Lust Behind Bars** and **Prison: School for Lesbians**.

Donn Pearce (1928 – 2017) was the author behind the book – and screenplay- which was turned into the classic prison-rebel film **Cool Hand Luke**. Having joined the Army in 1944 by lying about his age, Pearce hated the discipline and soon joined the Merchant Navy, sailing to Europe. Sensing quick money to be made, the young Pearce was arrested for passing counterfeit money and sentenced to work at an outdoor prison. He fled and made his way to Canada on a set of forged papers, and once back in the USA began another short-lived career criminal, this time as a safe-cracker. This culminated in two years on the chain-gang, which provided the raw material for **Cool Hand Luke**. Pearce never returned to crime, issuing several more novels before focusing on freelance journalism in the 1980s.

James Nelson Coleman (1940-97) wrote a pair of SF novels while in prison for most of the 1960s. Court papers are not clear unless you read legalese, but a combination of burglaries and fraud seem to have been his crimes, and he served at least some of his time in a Columbus Ohio Penitentiary. **Seeker from the Stars** and **The Null-Frequency Impulser** were both published by Berkley Medallion and by all accounts were uninspired SF-action.

Donald MacKenzie (1908–1993) was highly prolific, with 30+ books to his name, having also been highly-prolific as an international criminal, clocking up jail terms in the UK and America for crimes such as fraud and robbery. Much of this was documented in his auto-biographies **Fugitives** and **Gentlemen at Crime**, both of which were characterised with the droll humour you might have expected of a well-educated and travelled Englishman of that era. MacKenzie's debut novel, **Nowhere to Go** was made into a film by the famed Ealing Studios and his best featured a burglar called Macbeth Bain.

With thanks to David Avallone, Paul Bishop, Don D'Ammassa, Kev Demant, Lee Goldberg, Rob Matthews, Stephen Mertz, Linda Pendleton, Robert Randisi, Tom Simon and David Vineyard for their information and suggestions. As I go to press, I have received suggestions of another three authors eligible for this list, so will run a follow-up in issue 45.

Top - Russell Trainer drew on personal experience for sleaze titles such as The Warden's Wife and Denied.

Bottom - Michael Avallone's role in Thomas D Carroll's first of only two books is unknown, other than the dedication.

THE LOCKDOWN REVIEWS

Circus
by Alistair MacLean, 1975

"Dated compared with the ultra-violence and cynical anti-heroes so prevalent in US action-adventure of that period..."

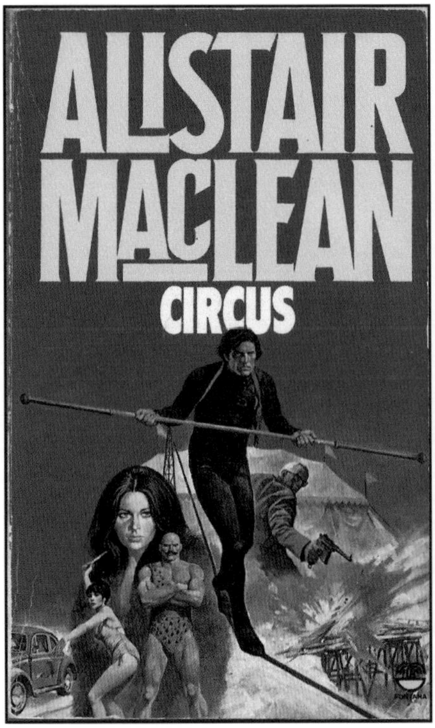

I had high hopes for Circus based on my only other MacLean reading, the high-octane WW2 thriller **Force 10 from Navarone**. However, despite sharing similarities in plot, this was a stodgy and convoluted read by comparison, dated by the standards of its publication year of 1975. A world-famous trapeze artist is recruited by the British Secret Services to tour his circus in the communist country of his birth, a front to use his talents to spring a scientist out of an impregnable prison-fortress. If the whole story had been focused on the escape attempt and the subsequent chase, it may have been much more exciting than its current structure, which flips the narrative to the events leading up to the break-out, detailing the romance and a murder-mystery amongst the circus troupe on the long voyage. The cast of quintessentially British gentlemen-spies and derring-do acrobats, as well as the budding relationships are charming by being so dated compared with the ultra-violence and cynical anti-heroes so prevalent in US action-adventure of that period. Perhaps MacLean was much more comfortable with period-settings such as World War Two rather than contemporary backgrounds. It was certainly well-reviewed at the time. I will read more MacLean, but I won't be looking forward to it as much as I had been before visiting **Circus**.

The Naked Soul of Iceberg Slim
by Iceberg Slim, 1971

"Any page you opened contained a phrase your parents wouldn't approve of.."

This is Robert Beck's fourth collection, a collection of excerpts, essays and letters issued as non-fiction. This was my first cover-to-cover encounter with his Iceberg Slim writings, although of course I am familiar with his importance as an African-American author and his wider influence on pop culture. I did find the world that Slim describes, and Slim as an individual in the auto-biographical sections, deeply shocking and disturbing. One erudite commentator had described Slim as the author of books in which any page you opened contained a phrase your parents wouldn't approve of. That was the Slim that I came in search of, and his coruscating ghetto-poet prose was scattered throughout this book, but more sporadically than I had hoped for, perhaps because of the nature of its variety of media, such as letters and essays. The piece that stayed with me was 'From a Steel Box to a Wicked Young Girl', the opening account of an ex-pimp's early days out of jail, where he professes to be too old for that profession and wants to leave it behind, but is gradually drawn back. It's not for the faint-hearted; "She left a Montana bordello to run afoul of a spermy gambler who ruined her commercial curves and blew away my heady dreams of mountainous greenbacks by blasting a squealer into her belly."

Nick Carter: Killmaster #2: The China Doll
by Michael Avallone and Valerie Moolman writing as Nick Carter, 1964

"They've got a bit of a goofy Sean Connery vibe that makes the whole 60s spy genre endearing..."

One of the longest running espionage series' in the Men's Adventure genre, the **Killmaster** entries are reputed to be very hit-or-miss depending on the author behind them. The series is also known for sporting several women behind the pseudonyms, notably Valerie Moolman, who wrote or co-wrote 11 entries.

This "Spy Chiller" finds our agent from AXE assigned to protect Soviet Premier Nikita Kruschev at a UN meeting, a routine job that almost went terribly wrong. After narrowly avoiding an international incident, he teamed up with a Russian agent simply named Comrade to infiltrate the Forbidden City in Red China and take out The Mandarin, a leader of the evil international organization CLAW, who is responsible for these attempted assassinations. In his hunt for The Mandarin, Carter runs through a gamut of 60s spy hijinx, including helicopter gunfights, Japanese bath house judo, a (no longer politically correct) Asian infiltration, and carnivorous snapping turtles.

I really like the Moolman entries, they've got a bit of a goofy Sean Connery vibe that makes the whole 60s spy genre endearing. Unlike other entries, the book moves along well enough and doesn't become boring. The action is sharp and the obligatory sex scenes are relatively modest, reflecting the time period. If you suspend your disbelief and just roll with it, you'll have a good afternoon with this entry. *Sean Nodland*

Nick Carter #39: Carnival for Killing
by Jon Messman writing as Nick Carter, 1969

"A crazy cat-and-mouse caper involving costumes, Cariocas, and cross-dressing..."

Nick Carter just wants to go on vacation. When he gets a call from the son of Todd Dennison, a friend of his, to look into some strange goings on at his plant in Rio, this seems like the perfect opportunity to get some R&R from the spy business and help out an old pal. However, AXE and the intrigue game has to muck up his plans. When he arrives in the country he's informed that his friend has been killed and it's up to Agent N3 to figure out who did him in and why.

This entry into the Killmaster series was penned by Jon Messman, whose entries are considered by many to be some of the best in the series. I really liked the first entry he wrote, **14 Seconds to Hell**. While the opening chapters were good, the whodunit that the first half consists of was contrived and very easy to see where it was going, regardless of the spoilers in the cover blurb that make it even more obvious. The second half, taking place during Rio's Carnival, made up for what the first half lacked. It was a crazy cat-and-mouse caper involving costumes, Cariocas, and cross-dressing that had just the right amount of silliness balanced tongue in cheek so as to not devolve into parody.

Messman does a good job in his writing though, bringing a level of quality that can be unfamiliar to this series compared to other entries. Action is swift and well executed, like the car chase in the first few chapters. One of the side characters, police chief Jorge, is a good supporting character to Nick and I enjoyed their scenes together.

All told, this book was not bad, however I was hoping for something similar to his previous instalment. The "mystery" in the first half was underwhelming but the second half was so much fun I did not really mind. Good for a Killmaster adventure, but not up to the previous bar set. *Sean Nodland*

PULP HORROR

The Mind Parasites
By Colin Wilson, 1967

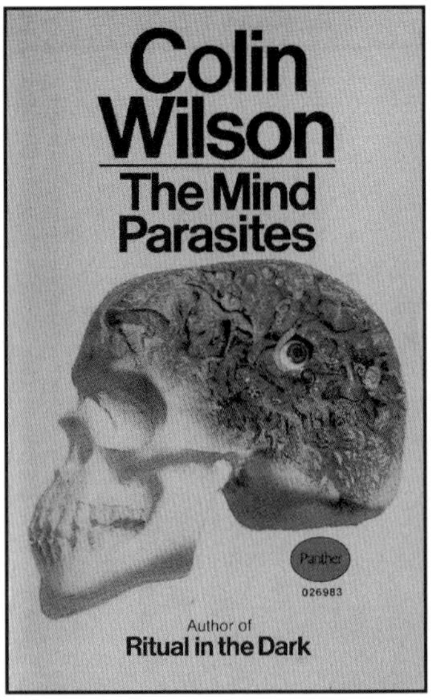

A brilliant and ingenious celebration of the power of the human mind wrapped up in an ingenious SF-horror package, The Mind Parasites is a dose of endorphins in paper format. Set in the near future and presented as a paper written by a leading academic, it's the story of a group of intellectuals who battle an alien race that lurk in the recesses of our mind, and whose malign influence have been responsible for the suicides, wars and murders that plague the planet. And the Cthulhu mythos, so it's not all bad. It is such a joyous read, and based on author Colin Wilson deep-diving into the minds of history's most evil men in much of his output, I was totally unprepared for such as a positive outlook on the potential of the human race. That Wilson attributes the negative aspects of our behaviour to an external force is a fascinating premise, and the way in which he weaves in the great philosophers and Lovecraft's Cthulhu mythos to the fabric of the story is remarkable. It reads like an updating of Eric Frank Russell's classic Sinister Barrier (1943) and an idealistic response to Robert Heinlein's rabidly anti-communist The Puppet Masters (1951). The perfect antidote to the COVID-19 blues.

The Sphinx
By Graham Masterton, 1978

I am a fan of Masterton's horror writing, especially his earliest works, but this is truly awful until the final few chapters. It is certainly missing Masteron's trademark everyman anti-hero who is plunged into supernatural peril against his will, and his ability to suspend a reader's disbelief by weaving together the impossible with the everyday and mundane. **The Sphinx**'s lead character is Gene Keiller, a handsome and ambitious career politician on the way up, who falls so in lust with a mysterious Egyptian beauty Lorie that he totally misses out on all the obvious clues that she is a were-lioness. What may have been intended as suave and seductive set of behaviours displayed by Keiller are by today's standards creepy at best, psychotic stalker at worst. I was willing for the clod to be devoured. The best character is a mysterious chauffeur/bodyguard whose tongue is missing but holds the key to Keiller's fate. I nearly guffawed at the scene where Lorie revealed that the huge bust Keiller has been lusting after is actually four pairs of breasts, and that her -ahem- mane is rather full.

Spore-7
By Clancy Carlile, 1979

A medical horror-thriller which combines George Romero's **The Crazies** with classic SF-horror **The Quatermass Experiment, Spore-7** is better than it has any right to be. The story's roots are in a highly infectious fungoid which turns law-abiding citizens into homicidal maniacs whilst destroying their body. I had assumed credited author Clancy Carlile to be a pseudonym as the writing was so good whilst the subject matter so schlocky, but there was a Carlile, and he went on to enjoy commercial success as a screen-writer when his later book **Honkytonk Man** was made into a Clint Eastwood film. Hollywood's gain was the horror genre's loss, as **Spore-7** has deft-characterisation, tight steering of the plot and a believable response from the authorities. An absolute gem of small-town horror, this reminded me of David Morrell's **The Totem**, which is one hell of a compliment.

PETER MCCURTIN

The Assassin #1: Manhattan Massacre
by Peter McCurtin

Yet again, we see an Italian American, well-versed in weapons, using his skills to take out mafia members in revenge for their killing of his family. Robert Briganti has got the usual characteristics - a good shot (from his work as a carnival shootist), access to heavy weapons (from his work with military surplus and the CIA), a single-minded hatred for Mob goombahs (from the drive-by shooting that killed his wife and son), and a penchant for cheating death as he delivers it (from the Men's Adventure logic that applies to all of these kinds of books). The story in this opening volume mostly involves him hunting down those directly responsible for the killing of his family, psychotic Don Coraldi and his goons. He hunts down lead after lead, taking him to the scummiest parts of New York City circa 1973, meeting some truly weird characters, before resolving the plot in an abandoned police station.

The griminess of the book is the biggest thing that I really took away from it. McCurtin manages to successfully make you feel like you are reading this in the back row of a 42nd Street grindhouse and trying to not think about what is making your feet stick to the floor. The locations are all seedy cesspits, from the hotels Briganti frequents, to the streets he walks down. The writing is top form, although it feels kind of different from his western and **Soldier of Fortune** books. He seems more focused on the character and his thoughts than he did in those, although that might just be me. The character of Briganti itself is pretty grim, claiming he's perfectly fine with killing innocents to reach his goal - although in the book he never does, opting instead for knockouts when they get in his way. The brutality he does display to those responsible is finely done, especially the beating that occurs early on that sets the tone for the violence to follow.

All in all, I enjoyed this book far more than expected. McCurtin delivers a stunning gut-punch response to Pendleton's work and there's no surprise it did so well. If you're looking for a vengeance tale that drags you through the back-alleys and abandoned slums of the big city (and I know you are), get this book. *Sean Nodland*

Sharpshooter #1 - The Killing Machine
by Peter McCurtin writing as Bruno Rossi 1973

The first entry into this **Executioner** clone, supposedly penned by Peter McCurtin himself, is a solid opening entry into a series with a convoluted history and a very mixed bag of entries.

The plot follows Johnny Rocetti, an Italian American businessman who loses his whole family, wife, parents, siblings, and in-laws, to Mafia violence. For their failure to acquiesce to the Mob's protection racket, the Rocetti family, sans Johnny, died violent deaths; the elders by a hand grenade and the rest in a hail of bullets leaving their funeral. It was after this attack that the titular character was born: Johnny Rock. Swearing vengeance, he pairs up with a Mafioso's widow, the lovely Iris, and sets to work causing death and disarray amongst the ranks of two rival families, the Farellis and the Albertos.

Curiously, the moniker for the character, "The Sharpshooter," is only referenced once in the novel, whereas Johnny refers to himself as The Enforcer (capitalization included) on several occasions in the novel. Perhaps this was a possible but rejected series title that never got washed out of the final draft?

I have some nagging doubts as to whether this book was entirely written by McCurtin himself. A lot of it reads like his writing: tight pacing, solid plotting, and a generally straightforward style of writing, but it seems to me to have too much specific detail for McCurtin. The author spends time, especially in the beginning, using specific brands of clothes, cigarettes, alcohol, and other unnecessary details, especially in the first half of the book. The gunfight scenes, while good, just don't really feel like his, there's not the same amount of oomph that you usually get. Not to say that this is any detractor, overall this is an above-average Mafia massacre tale that I would recommend to fans of the author-editor. *Sean Nodland*

NEW ENGLISH LIBRARY

Eat Them Alive
by Pierce Nace 1977

I though this book was quite good. It was competently written (high praise from anything coming out of Manor), and decently plotted. If this is your kind of thing, I think you would enjoy this. Despite its iconic status, I found the origin of the praying manti to be too implausible for my taste. But I'm sure that for most people who pick up a book about giant man-eating praying manti, a plausible origin story is not high up on the list of requirements. The pacing was uneven. The plot took a while to get moving, and then it read like the author realized he only had 30 pages to wrap everything up, and thus went into overdrive. I though Dyke had way too many resources easily at hand for someone who was supposed to be beyond the margins of society.

But these are quibbles. The real fault is that this didn't set up a sequel. Too bad. Can you imagine "Crab vs. Mantis?" They couldn't make enough paper to print the copies it would sell. *Scott Carlson*

Freaks
by Doug Lang 1973

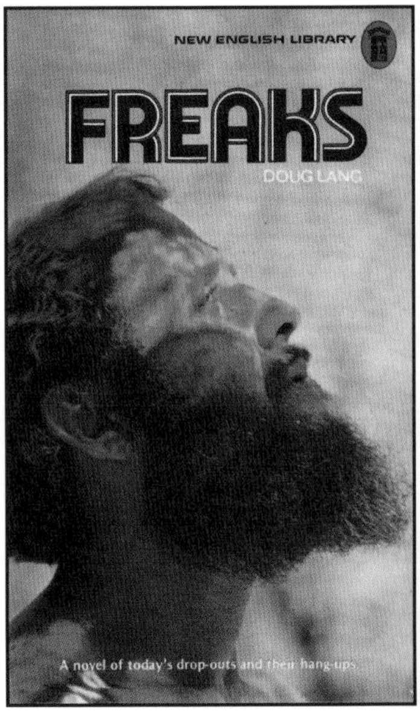

What the hell was that? First of all, it was short. It has 128 pages. But the story started on page 7, and it is has lot a very short (2 to 3 page chapters) with about a page of blank space in between. I would be surprised if there were 100 pages of content. What is is about? Drugs? Well, drugs are named dropped on nearly every page. But only rarely are the effects of taking said drugs touched on at all. Rock 'n Roll? Important rock musicians like Country Joe and the Fish, Johnny Cash, John Coltrane, Rachmaninoff and Schoenberg are named dropped, but with little comment beyond that. Poetry? The protagonist, Cal Longbow, is a poet, and we are treated to a little of his work. But there really isn't much interesting said about poetry. I don't think I learned anything about the early 70's poetry scene. Sex? Of course it's about sex. Most of the book is a monologue of Cal's sexual escapades. But it is not tawdry enough to be interesting, nor explicit enough for one handed Literature.

It was mostly about caricatures that I couldn't care less about. I was hoping at the end that giant crabs would emerge from the sea and devour them all. But no such luck. *Scott Carlson*

Jersey under the Jackboot
by R.C.F. Maugham, C.B.E., F.R.G.S., F.Z.S. 1946

This was originally published in 1946 and reprinted by NEL in 1980. What it gains from immediacy is lost by lack of perspective. The main point seems to be that the Germans were bad - thanks for the insight. I believe that some-one lower down the social scale could have gotten this point across even more forcefully. This was very badly dated. Still, I learned a few things reading this. I had no idea that the Nazi has run a research project on Jersey to create a race of giant crabs to use to attack England. Good thing the war ended before anything came of that. *Scott Carlson*

Wolfshead #1: Oath of Blood
by Ken Bulmer, writing as Arthur Frazier, 1973

"I entered into this book expecting a quick, rollicking Norman-Saxon combat tale..."

The first entry in this series follows shipwrecked Saxon Edric and a host of other characters, including his father, Ecgbert, and his Viking manservant, Beorn. They find themselves in the demesne of the Norman lord, Rolf du Lac, a friend of Edric's father. While being amicably held for ransom, Edric befriends the lord's son, Simon, with whom he finds a good sparring partner. He later falls in love with the Norman princess Ysabel and makes a bitter rival of Simon's malevolent brother, Odo. Through a series of drama-filled events Simon and Edric, once friends, become enemies in the first entry of this historically backgrounded tale.

I entered into this book expecting a quick, rollicking Norman-Saxon combat tale, however that's not exactly what I got. As such, I think I soured myself on this novel, however I will try to give it a fair shake. At a little over 100 pages of not-that-small type, this should have gone by quickly regardless of the quality, however the author absolutely stuffs this book full of characters, drama, and early Middle Ages politics. I had to reread sections to try and remember who was who, and the relationships between more than the central cast. Added on top of that was a sort of language the author used that can I can best describe as "high-falutin," trying to come across as more of an English dramatist than a pulp writer, while at the same time throwing in terms and verbiage of the time, something that would confuse and cause most readers to run to Google.

However, that did not get to me as did the utter lack of action. Except for the opening and closing combat scenes, the latter of which I felt was too short for what it was, there was barely any blood-soaked fighting.

This 6-book series was co-authored by Ken Bulmer and Laurence James, alternating novels between themselves. I can't find anything definitive online, but I'm going to assume this is one of Bulmer's entries and not James', as it's said that the latter would find the former's dearth of characters and plot lines from the previous novel too much to deal with and just kill people off and streamline the story.

By the final pages of it, which is when the promised Norman invasion occurs, this book really works more as a primer for a dramatic historical-fiction series. If that is what I thought I would be getting at the outset, I would have probably had a better outlook on the novel. As it is, I will give one of James' entries a shot, maybe he can deliver what Men's Adventure readers are looking for. *Sean Nodland*

The Marauders
Michael McGann, 1989

"This was a lot of fun, balancing an intelligent approach to the plot with outrageously OTT characters and action..."

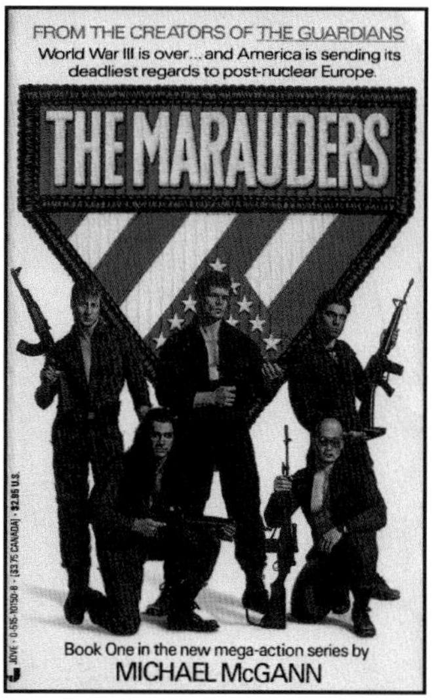

This was a spin-off to the popular post-apocalyptic series **The Guardians**, but based in Europe, with each episode detailing the titular's team mission in a different European country. This opening episode is split between KGB controlled London and the North Sea coast of Scotland, with The Marauders sent in to prevent the Russians using North Sea oil to fuel a blitzkrieg style attack on America. I do struggle with military-SF as it tends to be very right-wing, but this was a barrel-load of fun, balancing an intelligent approach to the plot with outrageously OTT characters and action. 'Shatterhand', the Scottish agent sent to work with The Marauders is a pure comic book creation, with a shock of ginger hair and a mutilated hand. One scene in which he butts heads with one of the Marauders is so full of homo-erotic tension that I expected them to start passionately kissing. Of course, they don't, instead forming an unbreakable bond based on their heroism and patriotism. The evil KGB overseer who is The Marauders nemesis is another excellent creation, totally ruthless but despairing of the British weather and the half-wit puppet King he has appointed. I was also pleasantly surprised at the fatalities amongst the main characters, suggesting the make-up of The Marauders would change from book to book, and introducing an element of tension. A well-told and slightly tongue-in-cheek entry to the post-apocalyptic team canon which passed the time very nicely.

Soldier of Fortune #7: Operation Hong Kong
by Ralph Hayes writing as Peter McCurtin, 1977

"A lot of the action is close and claustrophobic, gun and fist fights occurring in small Hong Kong rooms and halls..."

The book opens with our professional soldier Jim Rainey in Macao rather than Hong Kong, tracking down an antisemitic Frenchman named LaBeau, who killed an Israeli friend of his in cold blood. The aftermath of their encounter and the repercussions of it in the opening chapter lead our protagonist to the Crown Colony. There, he meets up with an old friend of his, Derek Philips, head of Hong Kong's Special Branch, to try and sell him some equipment. The meeting does not go as planned, of course, being interrupted by pro-communist bombing and rioting that badly injured them both. Following a very tense bomb-defusal and a personal attempt on his life, Rainey decides to head a task group to quell the Peking-organized unrest, organize pro-democracy counter-protestors, and root out the Red Chinese agents.

This entry in the long running series was penned by Ralph Hayes, who wrote 6 of the first 9 books published between 1976 and 1978, before being restarted in 1984 with photo covers. He emulates McCurtin's style well; he has more descriptions and details but not so much as to let his narrative drag any, while at the same time keeping up the hammering pace that our favorite editor made famous.

Hayes' action is as top-notch as ever, with the pace never letting up. He gives Rainey just enough time to grab a quick breath before he's forced to draw his Star .45 automatic. A lot of the action is close and claustrophobic, gun and fist fights occurring in small Hong Kong rooms and halls. I wasn't sure how well I'd like this entry and its more covert focus versus the earlier entries' traditional war narrative, but I was really blown away.

The only thing that took away from the narrative was a pretty skeevy sex scene in the beginning of the book. Normally sex scenes don't really bother me, even the less-than-PC ones, it's what you get with this kind of fiction. However not only is it basically forced, but Rainey even acknowledges that "She looked as if she had been raped, and that was not far from the truth." It just seems totally out of place to write it that way, even that line there could have been omitted and it would have come across a little better. *Sean Nodland*

CRIME AND PUNISHMENT

A Sense of Freedom
by Jimmy Boyle, 1977

The Enforcer
by Jack Burbridge, 1980

"Many fellow inmates and guards assumed Burbridge's sudden discovery of faith was a ploy to get early parole..."

Both Jimmy Boyle (b1945) and 'Happy' Jack Burbridge (b1938) developed their propensity for violence and criminality in the post war years, Boyle in Glasgow, Scotland and Burbridge in Mishawaka, Indiana. Each man subsequently went to prison in 1967 (Boyle had already done time previously) before then writing books about the moment their lives changed and they renounced their former behaviour. In Jimmy Boyle's case his epiphany took the form of exposure to art therapy whilst in HMP Barlinnie's notoriously experimental Special Unit for violent offenders, while for 'Happy Jack' it was a chance meeting with a Christian police officer when facing jail time that caused him to be 'born again' and to re-dedicate his life to God.

When Jimmy Boyle published his compelling 1977 memoir **A Sense of Freedom**, he was ten years into a life sentence handed down for the murder of William 'Babs' Rooney, a Glasgow underworld figure. Like Rooney, Boyle had grown up in the city's deprived Gorbals area, becoming by the early Sixties a serious protection racketeer and moneylender, notorious for the brutal punishments he handed out to rivals and backsliding debtors alike. The Glasgow that Boyle spent his youth in – hard weather, hard manual work, hard stone tenements, hard women and even harder men – comes across as more akin to Victorian Britain than being in any way like the sophisticated City of Culture Glasgow has developed into in more recent times.

The violence and brutality that were commonplace for Boyle out on the streets of Scotland's Second City continued uninterrupted when he was sent to prison. Banged up in Barlinnie in Glasgow but also in Nairn and Aberdeen nicks, Boyle developed a fearsome reputation whilst inside for assaulting staff and destroying prison property. Hardwired to fight back against all forms of authority, Boyle's time in jail before his transferal in the early 1970s to the 'Big Hoose's' Special Unit was marked by dirty protests and constant aggression towards and from staff, which left Boyle with, at different times, two broken arms and serious concussion. As **A Sense of Freedom** movingly reveals, the move to the Unit resulted in a huge change for the embittered con. Not only did he begin to read and write extensively, he also developed a talent for sculpture, following sessions with an art therapist who encouraged Boyle to channel his emotions into working with clay. After his release in the early 1980s Boyle continued to work as a sculptor and got married (to Sarah Trevelyan, a psychiatrist who had visited him whilst in prison). Together, they set up the Gateway Exchange, an arts rehab organisation devoted to assisting ex-offenders and drug addicts. **A Sense of Freedom** became the basis for a very good 1981 film of his early life and prison experiences directed by John Mackenzie and starring David Hayman as Boyle.

'Happy Jack' Burbridge enforced protection rackets for organised crime syndicates in the Midwest in the 1960s and also worked variously as a pimp and money lender. Every bit as brutal as Boyle (but favouring fists and guns over the Glaswegian's preferred weapon, a blade), Burbridge was, by his own admission, near-psychotic in his violent outbursts, maiming and crippling not just members of other crime families but even innocent passers by who happened to look at the perpetually grinning (hence the ironic nickname) Burbridge the wrong way. Finally busted in 1967 for armed robbery, Burbridge was facing twenty-plus years in Terre Haute Prison when conversations with committed Christian Lieutenant Commander Howard B Lytton of the Indiana State Police changed his life. Many fellow inmates and guards assumed Burbridge's sudden discovery of faith was a ploy to get early parole but in no time the ex-enforcer was setting up bible study groups in the cells and listening to visiting preachers.

Following his release, Burbridge worked with his former adversary, police officer Ralph Wolfe to set up a crime prevention scheme called 'The Cop and the Con' and spent time in jails talking to and converting those doing time. His memoir, **The Enforcer**, was published in 1980 by Christian publishing company, Acclaimed Books. Based in Texas, Acclaimed published other accounts of villainy and the saving power of the Lord (**Changed Lives in San Quentin**; **Holes in Time, the autobiography of a gangster** et al) as well as curios such as **Antichrist** by William S Rainey, 'Biblical technical advisor' to the makers of Omen II.

Jim O'Brien

I PREDICT A RIOT

Cage Five is Going to Break
By Richard E Johnson, 1970

"An assured bravado and conversational tone that feels authentic..."

The most interesting thing about the short novel **Cage Five is Going to Break** is that its author, E. Richard Johnson, wrote it while serving a 40-year prison sentence for his part in a robbery that resulted in murder. He wrote nearly every word of his 11 published crime novels from behind bars. Our main character here is Stacy Tate, a convicted bank robber incarcerated in Murphy Prison. Stacy is masterminding a breakout that involves several other inmates from his cell block along with his hooker girlfriend, Mae, working on the outside. She has access to the money from the bank job that landed Stacy in prison and is using it and her body to influence a susceptible prison guard. Almost the entire book is set-up as the reader is kept in the dark about exactly how this break will occur. We are introduced to an idealistic Custody & Treatment Officer, the cruel and sadistic captain of the guards, and the loser guard who becomes the target of Mae's end of the plan. Most of the prisoners remain simply names with the exception of Lucky Joe, a more than willing snitch if it can gain him some leverage on the inside. The entire book is well-written with an assured bravado and conversational tone that feels authentic. However, there is almost zero action and little suspense until the final 20 pages or so. I don't regret reading it, but I don't see myself seeking out further crime novels by Johnson with so many better examples of the genre available. *Steve Carroll*

Green River Rising
By Tim Willocks, 1994

"Unbelievably powerful and raw stuff..."

What if the warden of a huge Texas penitentiary were to go insane and not only incite a riot, but keeps its existence hidden from governing authorities in an attempt to allow it to escalate and run its course in order cleanse itself? And what if an unjustly convicted man, who is set to be released the next day after the riot begins, suddenly finds himself trapped inside? And what if that innocent man's love interest is in the prison's infirmary and no one knows she's there as the worst criminal elements in that prison population do everything possible to break into that infirmary to kill its dying patients and have their way with her? **Green River Rising** is a genuine epic in every sense of the word. Despite a single setting and a palpable sense of claustrophobia, the intertwining stories of the inmates and how they each factor into the plot as it spins fatalistically toward its conclusion is a white-knuckle ride like no other. This is unbelievably raw and powerful stuff, suffused with brutal violence and a profane world-weariness that adds a real sense of grounded realism to the events, even as it slowly embraces a larger than life and increasingly surreal nightmare quality. The book occasionally takes a pause to better inform a character's background or to expound a philosophical point, but it never comes to a stop; it is always hurtling toward its nihilistic conclusion and consuming the human carnage at every turn. It also happens to be beautifully written with descriptions that will have you re-reading entire paragraphs. But be forewarned, this book is the very definition of politically incorrect with regards to race, sex, identity, and gender roles. If you have a constitution strong enough to handle it, **Green River Rising** gets my highest recommendation. It is an unrelenting descent into literary madness that rewards those stern enough to tackles its pages. *Steve Carroll*

Underground
By James S Dutton Jr, 1977

"In a nod to the book's key influence, Baker stages any number of Rambo-style number of escape attempts..."

Part of the short-lived Scorpio imprint at Zebra showcasing writing from convict authors, Dutton's only novel was the the only one of that line to be packaged as fiction. It focuses on the character of Leslie Baker, a Vietnam veteran struggling with PTSD, who is sentenced to jail-time when mental health support would gave been more appropriate. At the whim of a prison governor, Baker is selected to be transferred to a top-secret and subterranean super jail which will house the most irredeemable scum of North America's penal system. In a nod to the book's key influence, Baker stages any number of Rambo-style escape attempts. With a fast-moving plot moved forward through dialogue, with little insight to character's motivations, it was reminiscent of the action/adventure books edited by Peter McCurtin at Belmont Tower Books in the early 1970s. This functional style of story-telling failed to pull me in, and it felt like I was serving a sentence with Dutton's no-frills one-off.

SCOTT GRONMARK

The Surrogate
By Nick Sharman, 1980

"Reminded me of the works of other British horror authors Graham Masterton and James Herbert..."

Frank Tillson, a talk-show DJ struggling to juggle his career and role as a single father, is contacted by his estranged father, a wealthy industrialist who is wasting away with terminal cancer. Despite the offer of riches that would solve his issues, Tillson refutes his father's overtures for a reconciliation, based on the cruelty he inflicted upon the young Tillson and his mother who was driven to suicide by the mental abuse she endured. However, even from beyond the grave, Tillson's father exerts his influence and if Tillson won't sell his soul for a shiny dollar, maybe his nine year old son will.

Gronmark's second horror book is certainly a more ambitious and intriguing effort than his debut, the written-to-order **The Cats**. I wouldn't totally agree with the views of Stephen King trumpeted on the cover, but there is one especially memorable sequence in this solid horror-thriller which raised goose-bumps by playing on a common childhood fear. I would have welcome more of this, but there is a lot to enjoy about **The Surrogate**, which reminded me of the works of other British horror authors Graham Masterton and James Herbert. Tillson's sheer bloody-mindedness and refusal to backdown reminded me of Herbert's working class and angry anti-heroes, and the weaving of real-life espionage and supernatural forces to drive a political outcome in **The Surrogate** reminded me of Herbert's **The Spear**. Masterton sprang to mind because Tillson's libido causes him real problems in one especially skin-crawling love scene, a device which Masteron invented, and the manner in which the hints to Tillson's father motives gradually reveal themselves through photos and phone calls, which is another Masteron calling card. Of course, being an early novel it doesn't hit the heights of either of those genre heavyweights, especially in the pacing and with much of the plot developments telegraphed in advance. But a great ending, quirky characterisation and a great premise means **The Surrogate** will provide you with a solid dose of chills.

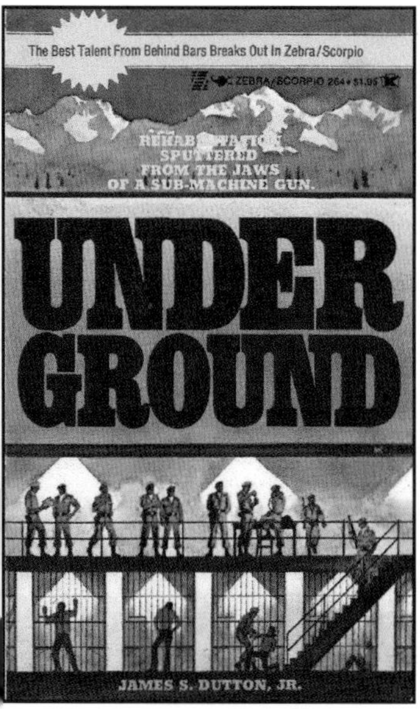

GIL COHEN HAS IT COVERED

The Executioner 15: Panic in Philly
By Don Pendleton, 1980

"Most will appreciate the snappiness of the narrative and the slickness of our protagonist..."

I read this entry in one sitting, on a flight from the UK to the US. It wasn't the circumstances of being stuck in a tube for almost 8 hours that made me do it, cause I would have done it again even if I was on solid ground, sitting on my porch. This isn't the only time I'd done this - I went through the European Adventures, **#5: Continental Contract** and **#6: Assault on Soho**, in an afternoon. For me, to blitz like the Man in Black himself through a novel is review enough and testament to the work of the late, great godfather of MA paperbacks. However, I think Justin would have a Panic himself if I just submitted those first three sentences as my review - although I also think he would sympathize.

For the uninitiated, **The Executioner** series is probably the longest, still running, series of Men's Adventure novels. They follow the adventures of Mack Bolan, a one-man-army fighting the Mafia after they led to the death of most of his family. His crusade leads him all over the country and occasionally overseas, bringing the spectre of Death to the Italian Underworld. This entry in the series sees him just outside Philadelphia, posing as a Family hitman to gain access to the Angeletti family's household. The heir apparent has been contracting goons from the Old Country to bolster ranks wrung dry by 'Mack the Bastard', who sees the danger in this practice spreading to other families in the US.

The book is pretty light on gunplay, only starting and finishing with it, but unlike other hack jobs that pursue the same tactic, Pendleton authors a narrative that hooks the reader in deep. The events only take place over the course of a day and a night, with Bolan expertly navigating the inner discord of the family while presenting himself to each member as an influential confidant, an outsider who can help each party attain their goals. I won't spoil the details, however I think most will appreciate the snappiness of the narrative and the slickness of our protagonist. There's no expansive depth to these characters, he is only there for a day after all, but I feel there's enough that Pendleton worked in to satisfy our readers. Pendleton's signature near-poetic prose is doing a great job peppering itself through the narrative illiberally, never becoming overwhelming.

The Maestro has hit another one out of the park and I'm kicking myself for not bringing another - however I should note that the next book, **Sicilian Slaughter**, was not written by Pendleton and is widely regarded as a hack job. The result of a row with the publishers, #16 isn't considered canon and is currently unavailable as a reprint and probably will never be. I plan on reading and reviewing it, albeit cautiously.

Sean Nodland

Printed in Great Britain
by Amazon

47442728R00037

THE YEAR OF THE COCK
#7
C.K. FONG
STREET VIGILANTE
VOYAGE OF DEATH
MARK CRUZ
CW00499191
THE SUPERSONIC ACTION STORY BY THE AUTHOR OF AIRPORT COP
CHARLES MIRON
AIRPORT COP
TWILIGHT STRANGLER
JOE BRODERICK'S WOMAN
JOHN H. ARBOR
HE SMASHED HIS WAY INTO THE UNDERWORLD TO SAVE THE WOMAN HE LOVED
CHECK FORCE
THE PEKING PLOT
China was the oldest civilization in the world-and was about to become extinct.
RALPH HAYES
THE ENFORCER is back and deadlier than ever.
Andrew Sugar
RALPH HAYES
WHEN THE CITY BECAME A JUNGLE, BRONSON HAD TO KILL FIRST TO SURVIVE.
CHECK FORCE
100 MEGATON KILL
Only two men - an American and a Russian - stood against the most bizarre conspiracy the world had ever known.
RALPH HAYES
THE JET-PROPELLED ACTION STORY BY THE AUTHOR OF AIRPORT COP
CHARLES MIRON
DEATH FLIGHT
#4 in a super-charged series!
ISRAELI COMMANDOS
THE ALPS ASSIGNMENT
Andrew Sugar
FIRST IN A BRUTALLY AUTHENTIC NEW SERIES.
KELLER
THE SMACK MAN
Someone was killing off hookers with bad dope. Keller didn't give a damn, but their bodies were cluttering up his precinct.
NELSON DE MILLE
FIRST PUBLICATION
THE ENFORCER is back and deadlier than ever!
#3 in a super-charged new series!
ISRAELI Commandos
The Kamikaze Assignment
Andrew Sugar
CHECK FORCE
SEEDS OF DOOM
The seeds of doom were planted, and Force III would reap the harvest of destruction.
RALPH HAYES
The toughest beat in the world—JFK International —and some days the action gets out of control
CHARLES MIRON
AIRPORT COP
"BREATHLESS, NAIL-BITING ACTION IS IN FULL FORCE!"
—Bestsellers
KILL SQUAD
DEAD END
MARK CRUZ
Like Kung Fu itself. Mace is silent, vicious, always deadly.
KUNG FU
MACE
THE YEAR OF THE BOAR
LEE CHAN
JOSEPH ROSENBERGER
Murder Master #3
OPERATION HOOKER
Hell was burning in Harlem and Lou King had to pose as a jive Mack Man to finger the boss pimp.
MR. DYNAMITE
TO KNOW IS TO DIE
C.H. GUENTER
MEET GANNON:
#1
He's after vengeance ... and leaves behind a trail of blood and gore.
Blood For Breakfast
DEAN BALLENGER
#1 in a super-charged new series!
ISRAELI Commandos
The Aswan Assignment
Andrew Sugar
"TOUGH AND EXPLOSIVE I LIKED IT."—ROBIN MOORE
MONDO
COCAINE KI
ANTHONY DESTE
DROP DEAD IN HAVANA
#2
GANNON
BLOOD FIX
OFF-DUTY THEY WERE CALLED...
KILL
JEFF ROVIN
HOLLYWOOD DETECTIVE:
THE WOLF
TIGERSHARK
KUNG

VIOLENT THOUGHTS

Welcome to the twelfth issue of **Men of Violence**. I really didn't expect to be typing those words in 2020, as this issue was totally unplanned (like my younger brother, but he must never know), but it kind of self-assembled itself over November and December. The trigger was a number of excellent contributions I had begun to receive from David "The Preacher" Wilson on the subjects of western and crime fiction. I was feeling guilty that I was unable to provide David with a likely date when I would be printing his work. I then realised I was in a similar situation with super contributions from Sean Nodland and Holger Haase, that I was also sitting on.

So for fear of becoming the fanzine equivalent of the lost **Dangerous Visions** SF anthology, which has been the subject of much acrimony over the decades, I decided to see if I could use their works as a spine for an issue of **Men of Violence**. Add in some sterling work from Paul Bishop, Stephen Mertz and Roy Nugen, and I had a self-assembled issue on my hands. And I have to say, the result is the most varied issue of any fanzine I have published in a while. I've had a blast working with the team on it, so I hope you get just as much enjoyment from reading it.

My own contribution is a look at Manor Books, a publisher which issued a number of collectible men's adventure series such as **Gannon**, **Keller** and **Bronson** to name a few. They are an outfit that fascinate me, operating in a semi-legit manner with rumours rife of Mafia ownership, and a shocking reputation for how they treated their authors. I've been collecting their titles for years now, and they have become increasingly challenging to find and afford. The pricing in particular is inverse to their quality, as so much of their output was mediocre at best. I plan to take a similar approach to some other lesser-documented publishers, such as Belmont Tower, in a forthcoming issue of **The Paperback Fanatic**, so I hope you like my approach.

I have also been busy working with thirty contributors on a second all-review special of **Men of Violence**, which will be themed around military fiction. It will carry over 200 reviews of paperbacks and comics set in the arena of war, and I am enthused about how it is shaping up. Expect to hear more in late Spring 2021. As a sneak preview, I have run a pair of reviews from Sean Nodland which were originally intended for its pages.

I hope that 2021 has got off to a good start, or at the very least is an improvement on the surreal hell that was 2020.

Regards.

Justin.

MEN OF VIOLENCE 12

Published January 2021

Dedicated to David "The Preacher" Wilson for turning up at just the right time

Thanks to the contributors-

Articles by Paul Bishop, Sean Nodland, Roy Nugen and David Wilson.

Scans from Lee Goldberg, Sean Nodland, Roy Nugen and Tom Simon

Proofreading by Tom Tesarek

Cover designed by Bill Cunningham

Cover painting by Raymond Kursar taken from his illustration for Bronson Streets of Blood

MEN OF VIOLENCE CONTENTS

MANOR BOOKS

28 GRINDHOUSE PUBLISHING
An overview of the renegade publisher Manor Books

31 MIND YOUR MANORS
A selection of Manor Books for your delectation

40 THE HARD EDGE
A visual guide to Men's Adventure series at Manor Books

44 FROM THE MANOR TORN
Stephen Mertz goes behind the doors of Manor to share a cautionary tale

FEATURES

6 NAM DOWN N DIRTY
Paul Bishop swoops in with The Black Eagle military adventure series

10 BE COOL ON THE LAM
David 'The Preacher' Wilson plays it cool with the Cool and Lam books

14 THE MALKO FILES
Holger Haase claims there are non-English language books worthy of discussion!

52 THE DEADLIEST GAME
Sean Nodland plays with the Soldier of Fortune series

INTERVIEWS

20 A BRASH ENDEAVOUR
David 'The Preacher' Wilson uses brute force to interrogate Lee Goldberg and Joel Goldman about Brash Books

58 ENTER THE MAQ
Bob Deis and Bill Cunningham put me out of business with their forthcoming publication

REVIEWS

4 DOUBLE WESTLAKE
David 'The Preacher' Wilson capers in with two of Westlake's crime comedies

49 THREE THE HARD WAY
David 'The Preacher' Wilson does hard time with the third of the Hardman series

62 BLAZING COMBAT
Sean Nodland blitzkriegs the final page with two military themed reviews

DAVID 'THE PREACHER' WILSON ON A PAIR OF WESTLAKE'S COMEDIC CRIME NOVELS

DOUBLE WESTLAKE

Somebody Owes Me Money

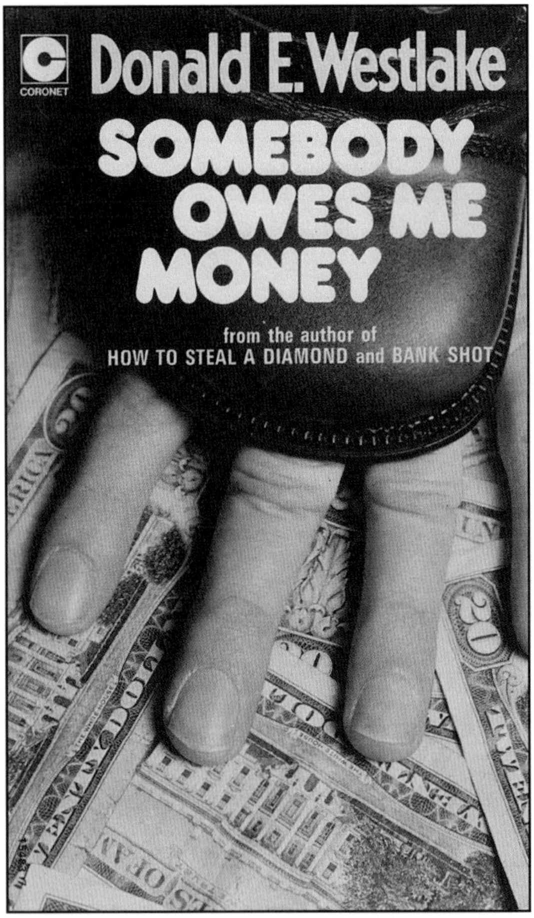

Donald Westlake wrote some classic comedic crime romps. Some are better than others, this one is fun, but falls short of the great humour I've come to expect. Most of his comedic material features crime capers falling apart in the most awkward manner. This novel offers a decent mystery, but its resolution seems to come out of left field after the author leads the reader on a strange and wacky journey through clues that have very little to do with the crime.

Chet is a cab driver who expects a nice tip from a passenger.

However, the passenger gives him a tip on a horse instead of a monetary tip. The bet is a longshot, but he places his bet with his bookie and wins big. However, when he goes to collect his winnings, he finds his bookie murdered. What follows is a comedy of mixups with cops, rival gangs, and a sexy blonde. It often seems reminiscent to a 1940's Bob Hope film.

The gangs each decide that Chet must be a hit man employed by the competing gang. The cops don't seem overly concerned one way or the other. Soon, Chet is being kidnapped, held prisoner, and even shot. All the while he is falling for the beautiful mini-skirt wearing blonde.

There are plenty of comedic moments in this title. I enjoyed Chet's thought process at one point where he considered "What would Robert Mitchum do?" One gangster is hiding in a closet and exposed by the cops. Because he didn't want to be found with a gun on his person he hides it inside a coat pocket and then forgets he has done so, leaving the gun behind.

When we finally get to the resolution, once again, that scene takes on the appearance of a 1940's mystery. All of the suspects are brought into the same location-- like one would see in a Charlie Chan or Thin Man movie. However, none of the suspects in the room are anybody that the reader has been looking at for 90% of the book. That resolution made me feel that Westlake wasn't playing fairly with the reader and really hurt the story for me.

Still, overall, I enjoy Westlake's books.. They just can't all be home runs. This one is more like a double-- fun, but falling short of greatness.

3 stars

"In order to fully enjoy this comedic romp one has to remove his thinking from reality to an extent. We can do it for comic books and fantasy books, why would we not do so for comical crime novels?"

Help! I'm being Held Prisoner

Nobody writes funnier crime stuff that Donald Westlake did. This time around, it's not the usual "Dortmunder" crew, but instead a whole new gaggle of crooks. Harry is a nice guy, but he has a German last name that is often mispronounced as a vulgar name for a woman's private parts. As a youngster he develops a defense mechanism-- he becomes the ultimate practical joker. That misguided sense of humor leads to a huge practical joke that results in a multi-car accident that results in a number of injured people and a couple of embarrassed congressmen.

Hence, the law throws the book at him and he winds up doing a 2-3 year stint in prison. Once there, because he is not a violent offender, he gets offered "special duty" that has very little check-in, etc. and discovers that his fellow workers have a way out of the prison. Not that they want to break out, but instead, they are running a **Hogan's Heroes** type operation from the prison-- committing crimes with the perfect alibi-- "We were in prison." They soon bring Harry in on their plan to rob a couple of banks-- but Harry is a non-violent offender and not anxious to become involved in such a scheme.

From that point on Harry has to use every practical joke in his book in order to try to keep the robberies from taking place. In an effort not to be discovered by his fellows, he tries to keep his practical joker past from becoming exposed and keeps thwarting the robberies with tricks like dropping a stink bomb in the bank, calling in a bomb scare, etc. Harry will do anything to keep from actually having to hold a gun on someone.

Enter another problem. Someone in the prison keeps playing practical jokes by finding ways to send a message that says "Help! I'm being held prisoner!" The warden keeps thinking it is Harry because of his practical joking past. This keeps getting him in trouble with the warden. Being in trouble with the warden might make his "gang" think he is ratting them out.

In order to fully enjoy this comedic romp one has to remove his thinking from reality to an extent. We can do it for comic books and fantasy books, why would we not do so for comical crime novels? The author keeps the predicaments, and the jokes coming. The reader keeps looking to see if the robberies will get committed and trying to figure out who keeps sending the notes. This all builds to a fun conclusion as we discover Harry is not the best practical joker in the prison. It isn't hard to figure out who the real joker is, but it is fun watching Harry and the warden struggle over the messages.

This is a very pleasant book and I enjoyed it just about as much as I enjoy the Dortmunder series by this author. From page one, the reader is treated to comical pacing, clever concepts, and fast quips. This one is a treat from the beginning until the very clever conclusion.

4 stars

PAUL BISHOP SWOOPS IN WITH A BIRDS-EYE VIEW OF THE BLACK EAGLES SERIES

'NAM DOWN AND DIRTY

There were numerous old school men's adventure series which used the Vietnam War as a background. Two of the best were **Saigon Commandos** and **M.I.A. Hunter**. The Black Eagles isn't quite in the same league, but with twenty-one titles it's one of the longest running military action-oriented men's adventure series. The Black Eagles also sported cool thematic cover art, which was kept consistent for the entire run—a feature valued by collectors.

Published by Zebra between 1983 and 1990, **The Black Eagles** books were written by several different authors under the pseudonym John Lansing. As a result, the merit of the stories swings between mediocre and very good, with a couple of excellent entries. It was often Zebra's editorial policy that hurt the series by insisting on a high page count. This meant 180 pages of solid story had to be padded out to 250 pages of small print.

The highly revered men's adventure writer William Fieldhouse, was the power behind **The Black Eagles**. He is perhaps best known for creating Gold Eagle's **Phoenix Force** series under the pseudonym Gar Wilson. **Phoenix Force**, along with **Able Team**, were series spin-offs from Gold Eagle's highly successful The Executioner series—the big daddy of all men's adventure paperback originals. Phoenix Force ran for fifty-eight titles, thirty-two of which were written by Fieldhouse. He is considered 'the' Gar Wilson, by serious **Phoenix Force** fans and collectors.

Prior to **Phoenix Force**, Fieldhouse wrote for **The Executioner** series. He also wrote numerous standalone and series Westerns (**Klaw**, **Six-Gun Samurai**, **Gun Lust**, etc.) and other contemporary action novels under numerous pseudonyms (**M.I.A. Hunter**, **Stony Man**, and others). Along the way, he created and wrote the military action series **The Hard Corps** under the pseudonym Chuck Bainbridge.

Fieldhouse created **The Black Eagles** series when he was approached by Zebra to create a house name series about the U.S. military during the Vietnam War. Fieldhouse recalls: I was not keen on this. I'm an Army veteran, but I wasn't in Vietnam. However, when I was taking BCT at Ft. Jackson, they started pulling troops out of Nam. The veterans of that 'conflict' had usually been depicted in a very negative manner (demented kill-crazy psychopaths or maybe psychotic). I figured I might be able to portray U.S. troops in Nam in a more positive manner. I was already writing two series. Really didn't want another house name project. So I came up with basic format, characters and so on, acceptable by the publisher, and farmed out the actual writing to three individuals.

"The Black Eagles books were written by several different authors under the pseudonym John Lansing. As a result, the merit of the stories swings between mediocre and very good, with a couple of excellent entries..."

This was much the same process Stephen Mertz used when creating his **M.I.A. Hunter** series. Both Mertz and Fieldhouse were expected by their publishers to ensure the books were of publishable quality and to do any rewriting required. This often led to a considerable amount of unexpected work. Due to the long running success of **The Black Eagles** this rubbing point was exacerbated, demanding far more effort on Fieldhouse's part than he originally envisioned. In referring to the writers he chose, Fieldhouse stated: One was a good writer with an extensive military background. Another had a track-record, but also had extremist views (political and

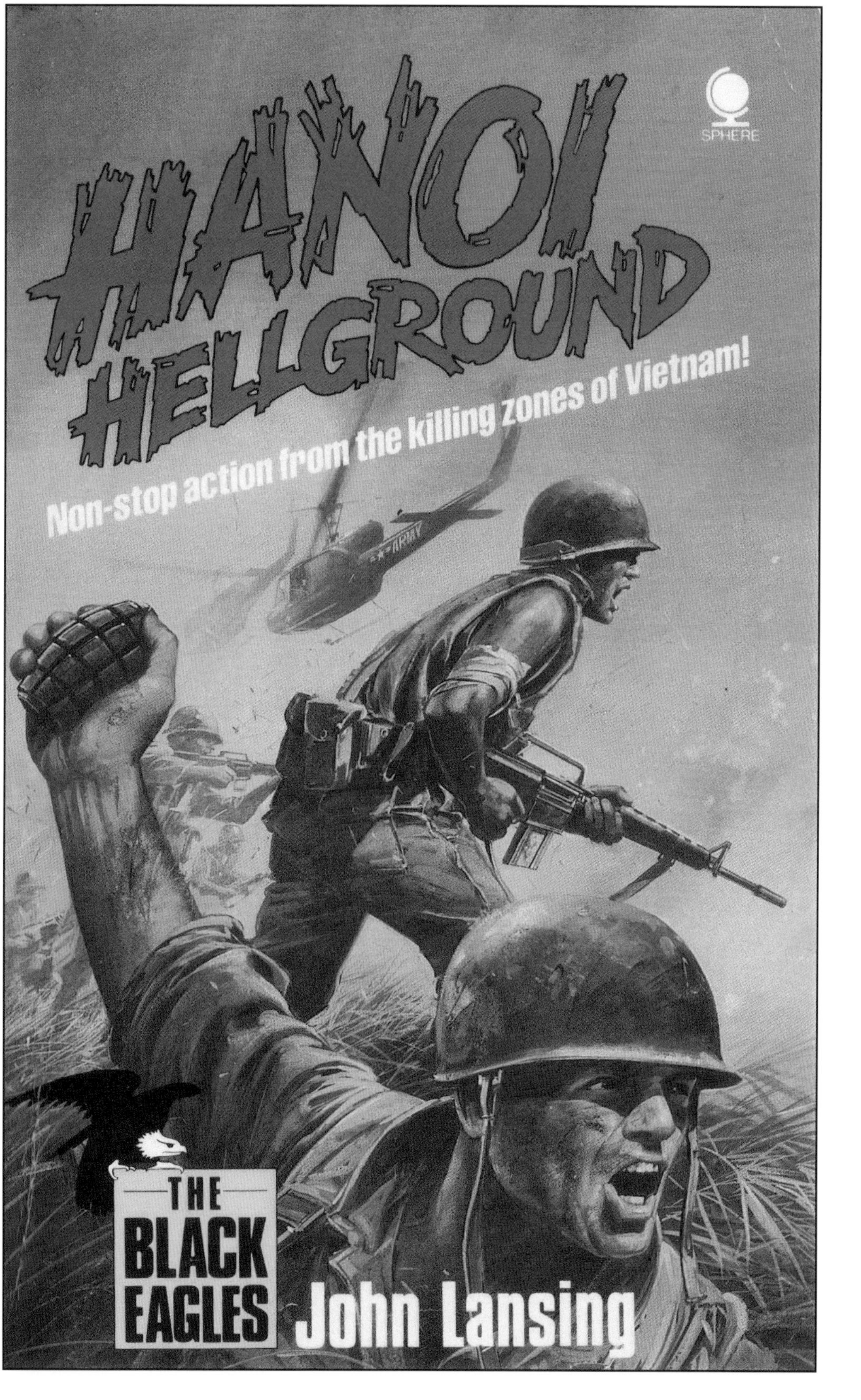
SPHERE
HANOI HELLGROUND
Non-stop action from the killing zones of Vietnam!
ARMY
THE BLACK EAGLES
John Lansing

otherwise) that steadily became more obvious in his work. The third was quite intelligent, but inexperienced as a fiction writer.

The first entry in the series, **Hanoi Hellground**, was written by Mark K. Roberts, an experience pulpster whose credits included the even numbered entries in **The Penetrator** series and four volumes in the jingoistic **Soldier For Hire** series. Under the house name Patrick Lee, Roberts had also contributed to the **Six-Gun Samurai** series, for which Fieldhouse also wrote. Along with an off-kilter (and often inappropriate) sense of humour, Roberts had a penchant for overdoing Tuckerizations—the naming of characters after many of his writer friends. Politically to the right of Joseph Rosenberger (of **Death Merchant** fame—or infamy), Roberts would also indulged in rants about his views to pad out his page count. Later, Roberts would create and write the **Liberty Corps** series, another military oriented men's adventure genre entry.

It was Patrick E. Andrews, however, who wrote most of the remaining **Black Eagles** books. An Army brat growing up, Andrews enlisted in the Army at age nineteen. He served as a paratrooper in the 82nd Airborne Division in the active Army and the 12th Special Forces Group Green Berets in the Army Reserves. He left military service after being injured in a parachute jump.

After the Army, Andrew's worked as a typesetter in San Diego while sending manuscripts to numerous publishers without success. He then became a technical editor and writer in aerospace while still pursuing his fiction writing. Eventually, he began to get published (like Fieldhouse and Roberts, he also wrote for the **Six-Gun Samurai** series). He went on to write more than fifty novels in the men's adventure, military adventure, Western, and historical genres. Andrews writes in a breezy but his military background, however, kept his entries rooted in solid believability.

Paul Glen Neuman wrote only one **Black Eagles novel**, **AK-47 Firefight**. Neuman had previously written seven **Phoenix Force** books, as well as two entries in the notorious **They Call Me Mercenary** series (#16 **China**

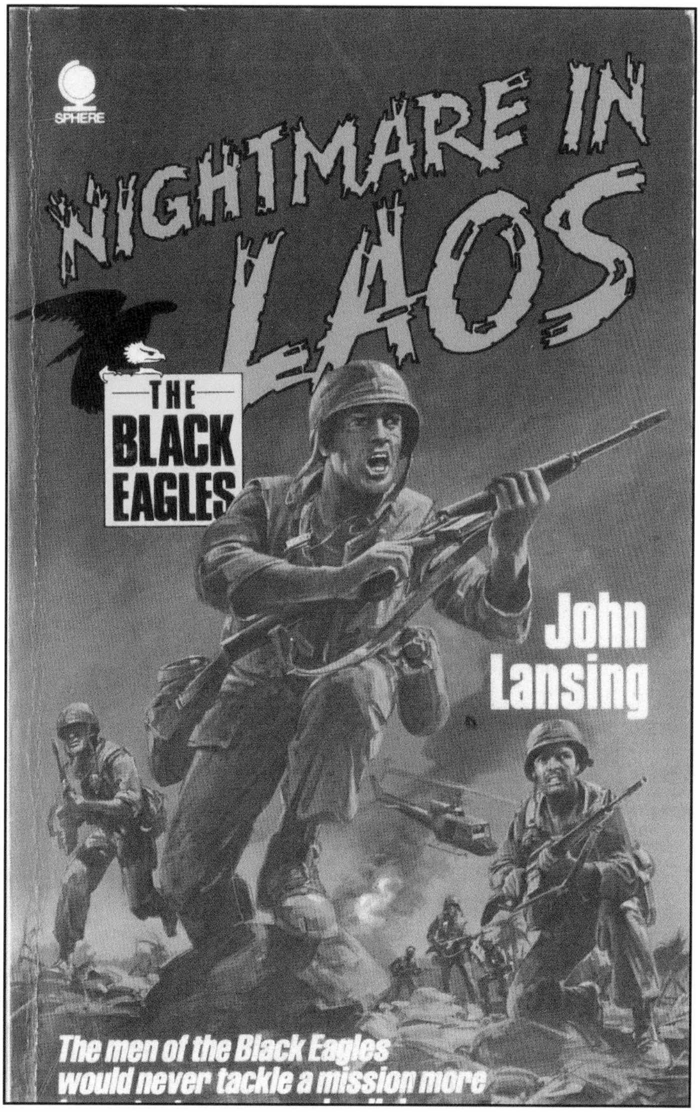

Blood Hunt and #17 **Buckingham Blowout**). Calling it grunt work, Neuman stated **AK-47 Firefight** was written under a tight deadline of six weeks for the book's approximate 240 pages. Personal interviews conducted with veterans of the War provided an insight, which proved invaluable for the novel's authenticity.

> **"One was a good writer with an extensive military background. Another had a track-record, but also had extremist views that steadily became more obvious in his work. The third was quite intelligent, but inexperienced as a fiction writer."**

David Cheney, who wrote at least two and possibly as many as four **Black Eagles** entries, is a bit of an enigma. A pharmacist in the San Diego Area for over thirty-eight years, he left the men's adventure genre behind after writing for **The Black Eagles**. His only other publication appears to be a 2014 sci-fi novella, **Mars—The Deep Con**.

Despite the varied quality of the series, **The Black Eagles** is worth both reading and collecting. It is a prime example of the military sub-genre under the men's adventure masthead.

DAVID 'THE PREACHER' WILSON LOOKS AT THE A A FAIR BOOKS AND THEIR DETECTIVE AGENCY ODD COUPLE

BE COOL WHILE ON THE LAM

A.A. Fair was one of the pen names used by Earl Stanley Gardner, the creator of famed fictional attorney **Perry Mason**. He wrote nearly 100 mystery novels, all of which sold at least 1,000,000 copies. For many years, he was the best-selling author in America. His A A Fair novels featuring the detective team of Donald Lam and Bertha Cool ran to 32 books across a period from 1939 to 1970.

Lam and Cool both show signs of a common creator, being cut of the same bold cloth with some distinctions. Bertha Cool runs a detective agency and Donald Lam is her partner. Despite her name, she is anything but cool. She is excitable, greedy, and complains about anything and everything. A stout woman who resents a woman who uses her good looks to achieve her ends.

Lam is a clever detective who appears to be almost a lamb compared to the stereotypical private eye type as he quietly pieces parts of the puzzles together and then cleverly reveal the proper culprit. The revelation of these mysteries always leaves the reader wondering how they did not see the same solution that Lam did. He is mocked for being short by the cops and he refuses to carry a gun.

In fact, a feature of almost every one of these novels includes the obligatory scene where Lam gets jumped and beaten. In **Count of 9** (1958) Bertha asks Lam why he won't just buy a gun and he tells her that he would have to replace his gun every time he gets jumped and beaten. But he is anything but a lamb. In at least one of these novels Lam, despite his diminutive size, is off fighting World War II.

In the ninth entry to the series, **Cats Prowl at Night** (1943), and the earliest of the series I have read, Donald is vacationing in Europe, a euphemism for being in the war, since the copyright date in the jacket would fit this timeline. I know that other novels referenced him as having served. I think, if I recall correctly, Lam saw enlisting as his duty and Cool disagreed, and therefore she sarcastically refers to it as a vacation until he returns. So, I think the reference to vacation is an inside joke, perhaps between Gardner and a friend, but most certainly between Bertha and Donald.

Bertha is determined to resolve a case, she smells money, but it is not long until the case becomes one of those old-fashioned puzzles with half a dozen suspects. By today's standards I would have become more and more angry at each introduction of new characters who are possible suspects, but for 40's gumshoe stuff it is par for the course. With Lam missing in action for this case the author is forced to fill it up with something and he decides to add possible suspects.

This one is quite readable. There is a hugely comic scene when Bertha consults with her attorney that Perry Mason himself would have been chuckling over.

This is not a great mystery, but not a bad one, either. Worth reading for its style, its nostalgia, and its main characters.

In the thirteenth entry, **Fools Die on Friday** (1947) the pacing is almost frenetic-- moving rapidly along from scene to scene-- with a sense that something needs to be done quickly. The author moves gracefully from plot twist to plot twist. The client comes to Lam and Cool seeking protection for a businessman whose household she serves as a secretary. She believes he is to be poisoned. Lam immediately suspects it is a setup to create a frame for someone. He arranges a plot that he calls "psychological handcuffs" to keep the wife from poisoning her husband. To Lam's dismay the husband is actually poisoned, and the plot is off to the races from there. This novel features a rather eccentric cast of characters: a dentist, a conniving wife, a grumpy butler/driver, a sexy business woman, a gambler with a system for betting the horses, a fired dental assistant, and of course, the law is represented by Sergeant Sellers, who is trying to solve the mystery himself.

"Bertha Cool runs a detective agency and Donald Lam is her partner. Despite her name, she is anything but cool. She is excitable, greedy, and complains about anything and everything. Lam is a clever detective who appears to be almost a lamb compared to the stereotypical private eye type."

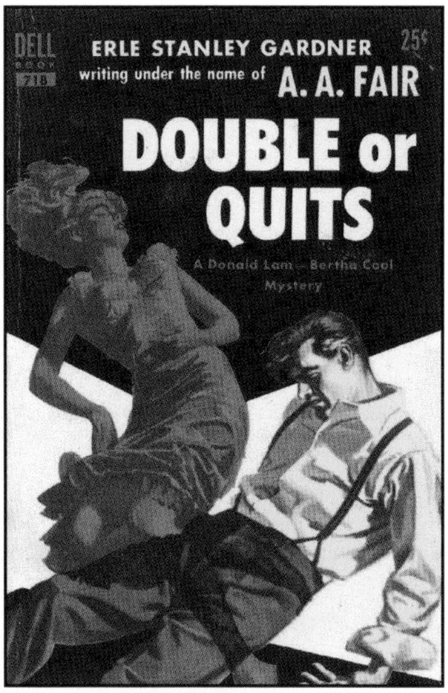

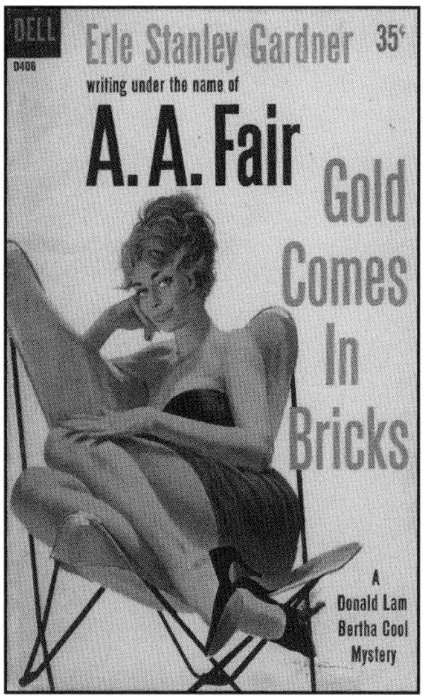

Gardner writes clever stories. Nothing is ever as it exactly seems.

Every character has his or her own agenda. Most have their own secrets that complicate the murder mystery. Through it all, Lam connives, plots, searches, and sets his own traps while avoiding falling into the hands of the police and preventing them from using the framed-up evidence against his client or others.

Lam is a sucker for the dames-- seemingly falling in love at the drop of a hat. Funny that the women in these books always have "nice legs" or a "nice front." I do not remember an ugly character (with the exception of Bertha, who might not be ugly, but the author conveys a certain unattractiveness). Despite the fact that women can be a sort of Kryptonite, Lam has a strange appeal to the ladies. It seems that they all want to get close to him. Even though just about every woman seeks to manipulate him, he picks and chooses the women he will actually help. That does not

mean he always chooses well. He can be both sympathetic and hard-boiled. He can be either susceptible or immune to their charms.

The dialogue is a bit dated. Bertha's favourite exclamation is "Fry me for an oyster!" There is a bit of a side story involving horse race betting that adds to the fun. As long as the reader remembers that this book is set in the 1940's, he will enjoy a step back in history, style, and flavour. Modern writers try to recapture this era from time to time-- but none of them are a substitute for this author, who is the real thing.

The twentieth entry was a well-crafted mystery, **The Count of 9** (1958), in which the agency was hired to guard a party held by a wealthy travel writer/adventurer. At an earlier party, a jade Buddha statue was stolen, and the writer doesn't want a repeat. Even though Bertha was present and alert, a blowgun was stolen along with another jade Buddha. Never fear, Donald knows how to get on the trail. In a miraculously short period, Donald can figure out how the items were smuggled out, retrieve them, and begin to return them to the owner. He does return the blowgun but is concerned that the actual thief is either the man's wife or her friend and holds the Jade Buddha back until he can meet with the writer in person. Of course, the writer is murdered with a poison dart, and Lam finds himself working to find the killer.

This story is enhanced by being what amounts to a locked room murder mystery. When the murderer is revealed the reader is left with the impression that Lam figured it out long before he explains it to the police. The adversarial relationship that the agency has with the police department, in particular homicide detective Frank Sellers, is a bit of a love-hate relationship. Detective Sellers always holds the opinion that Lam is holding back information and he usually is correct.

Bachelors Get Lonely (1961) is the twenty-third entry to the series so one of the later instalments, and without being "dirty" it is in some ways just a little racier than the others. Lam has his secretary cutting out articles about crime sprees with the thinking that he might find a way to use some of the incidents as a "cover" for some of his investigations. In fact, articles about a Peeping Tom play an important part in solving this mystery. Soon, he is embroiled with some of the standard material we see in this series. Lam manipulates or is manipulated by women, plays upon legal technicalities, and finds himself a suspect in a murder. Finally, he contrives a way to use the newspaper stories to set a trap. As usual, nobody is exactly what they seem.

This is another fun outing from an author who knows how to write a fun story.. One of the cool things about Lam is that though he is good looking and smooth with the women, the cop continually calls him "pipsqueak" or “pint-size” which suggests he is nothing physically big. This makes the material even more fun because Lam is not your typical hard-boiled private eye. He is a thinker and a manipulator. He gets roughed up in almost every book.

In this instalment, the cop, Sellers, provides some of Lam's roughing up when he commits an act of police brutality that lands him in a little hot water. It is important to remember that this was the period in which a lot of excesses of police powers were being ruled on in courts for the first time. It was normal for confessions to be taken from suspects using brute force and coercion. Sellers intends to do exactly this to Lam. As they discuss evidence rules the cop complains that the courts are taking handcuffs off the crooks and putting them on the police. To some extent, this was true, and it is and was the attitude of many law-and-order people. While these rulings were necessary to remind us of the rights of the accused, it added some realism to the story to have the officer wrestle with it. The right to remain silent was known to some people, but the police were not yet required to advise people of their rights and were less respectful about protecting those rights. The way these concepts are presented make the story more realistic and in keeping the story moving forward. A fine novel and a solid mystery.

These novels have some of the Perry Mason feel without the courtroom interrogations. They are clever mysteries packed full of the usual cross and double-cross. Despite their age they still offer adequate punch for the modern reader.

The Preacher star ratings out of 5

The Count of 9 ****

Cats Prowl at Night ***

Fools Die On Friday ***

Bachelors Get Lonely ***

DOUBLE AGENT HOLGER HAASE, A GERMAN LIVING IN IRELAND, LOOKS AT FRENCH LANGUAGE BOOKS TRANSLATED INTO GERMAN.

THE MALKO FILES

The Malko series is what I would call an iceberg character, in that the number of English language volume is just the tip of the iceberg. In France, the home country of Malko's late creator Gerard DeVilliers, the series ran to hundreds of entries. It was also translated to other European languages, including German, which is the source of the material for this piece.

Malko 59 – Rockets against Venezuela

Let's face it: Most of my literary and cinematic obsessions from an early age on were based on English language creators so when I moved from Germany to Ireland all those years ago, one of the welcome by-products for me (especially in that pre-Internet age) was easier access to some of my favourite writers and film makers.

The flip side of that coin however, only became apparent to me over time: Foreign language material is woefully underrepresented in pretty much all English language markets. And this is twice a challenge for foreign language books. For films you could just source a subtitled niche market DVD or Bluray but if you do not understand the book authors' languages how are you ever going to familiarize yourself with them?

On the continent we are used to having a large selection of foreign language books available to us in translation. When Patrick Modiano won the 2014 Nobel Prize in Literature it generated a widespread "Who he?" in Anglophone countries though I had already read some of his work as it is very easily available in German translations (and in most other European countries). When Umberto Eco was still alive, I always got his books in German as the English translations often appeared much later. And Walter Kempowski's **Homeland** took nearly three decades before it was available to English language readers.

"Gérard de Villiers' massively successful series of French language SAS Spy novels around impoverished Austrian prince Malko Linge who regularly accepts high paying espionage gigs in order to afford the upkeep of his castle and lifestyle"

The list is endless.... Fact is that if you rely on English language books you are way less exposed to foreign literature than readers in other countries.

And if you think this only applies to "highbrow" literature look at pulp or genre fiction.

Case in point: Gérard de Villiers' massively successful series of French language **SAS** (short for Son Altesse Sérénissime = His Most Serene Highness) Spy novels around impoverished Austrian prince Malko Linge who regularly accepts high paying espionage gigs in order to afford the upkeep of his castle and lifestyle. #firstworldproblems... I know.

In French, the series reached 200 novels published from 1965 until the author's death in 2013. Of those four were published in 1969/70 for NEL (under the original SAS series name) and another 15 in the mid-1970s for Pinnacle (as a series of **Malko** and later Malko: Spymaster novels). It's only recently that Vintage Crime/Black Lizard revisited this literary franchise again at last and published a number of the later Malko Linge novels such as **Chaos in Kabul** or **Madmen of Benghazi**.

In comparison to this 139 of those were printed in Germany between 1977 to 2001 by Cora, a publisher who specialised in "Heftromane", 60+ page pulp novels that are available through newspaper kiosks, not in regular bookstores. And even though the Malko novels were regular sized paperbacks they could mainly be found in train stations or similar outlets.

Whereas a large part (though not all) of the English language **Malko** books at the time featured hand drawn cover images, the style of the German covers was clearly inspired by the French series which showed photos of scantily clad ladies with the **SAS** series logo superimposed in the top half of the cover and author's name and book title underneath. The German books had different girls in various stages of undress but shot in the same style under a capital M (for Malko) below which we have the series title Malko (as opposed to SAS), the book title and name of the author.

I vividly remember the first time I read one of the Malko books. I was in my early teens and I was sucked into buying this book by the image of a hot model on the cover with an Afro haircut and a machine gun in her hand. And right on the first page I was being introduced to a Middle Eastern character with such an opulent lifestyle that he used to just discard his luxury watches when they needed to be wound up again but now made some concessions and inisted on having his servant wind them up for him to be ready at his bedside in the morning.

It was only decades later when I revisited the series that I discovered it was from **Kill Kissinger** (Pinnacle's **Malko** #6), the 34th entry in the original French series and that the German version (**Attentat auf Kissinger**) had actually been the debut in that market.

Gérard de Villiers was a well-travelled journalist and French Counter-Espionage officer with a wide range of contacts in the diplomatic and intelligence field. Malko was created when the death of Ian Fleming had left a void for this kind of genre and de Villiers was encouraged by his editors to try his hand and create a similar character. And what he ended up creating was a James Bond type by way of a Jess Franco movie, where all the Bond traits are clearly recognisable though often cranked up to the n-th degree with more violence, sex (and sexism) and often hardcore right wing points of views, staunchly anti-communist as well as often racist. And yes, women in his novels often do enjoy being slapped. Rape scenes are de rigueur, and the victim does not always seem to loathe the experience.

For all the trash factors that can be found in his books, they also are incredibly well researched. It is obvious that the international locations are written by someone who has either been there or was well briefed by people who knew the areas very well. The drama is always contemporary and at times even prescient. Once you remove the obvious fictional layers of the books and with a distance of often a few decades behind us now, some of the publications are even fascinating time capsules. **SAS versus the CIA** e.g. is one of the only works of fiction that I can recall describing in vivid detail a very modern pre-Revolutionary Iran under the Shah.

For all the countries Malko has visited over all the years, there is one place he appears to have never engaged in..... France, the home of his creator. De Villiers once mentioned that this was in order to protect his own intelligence sources. And just like Kennedy was a fan of Fleming, Malko appears to have been a favourite for Jacques Chirac and Valéry Giscard d'Estaing.

Over the years the character has featured in two movies and a series of comic books and it seems that a new series of **Malko** movies may soon be due starring Michael Fassbender. While he would be a good choice in the title role, I strongly suspect that this would end up an incredibly watered-down version of the original character. As even James Bond is constantly being criticised for being an outdated sexist type and his films becoming increasingly unwatchable, I just cannot imagine anyone these days faithfully adapting Malko, a book series that is often way more over the top sexist and violent than any of the Bond books they were obviously inspired by.

Though for a while most (if not all) of the French books were translated into German four times a year, the order was slightly different. As such SAS #67 **Rouge Grenade** (**Red Grenade**) became Malko #59 **Raketen gegen Venezuela** (**Rockets against Venezuela**).

And contrary to the German title, little to nothing in the book actually has anything to do with Venezuela. There is a threat against that country but that is more of a McGuffin and comes from Grenada where most of the plot is based.

After a local resident and member of the British Secret Service steals a secret document revealing a deal made with the Cubans to station mid-range weaponry on the island threatening neighbouring Venezuela, he gets captured and brutally tortured and killed before he can reveal the whereabouts of this paper. Malko's CIA contacts recommend him to the MI5, the British domestic security service that we learn is indeed responsible for the countries belonging to the Commonwealth: He is to visit the island in the guise of an ordinary tourist and businessman together with a striking female Venezuelan spy as his partner and try and uncover the location of those documents.

Though all the German Malko novels featured stunning looking girls with very little clothing on their covers, this book appears to be the only one to also feature some nipples poking through a see-through bodysuit. Nudity at German newsstands in the 70s and 80s was not uncommon (compare this with the puritan attitude displayed by modern social media) but my hunch is that the publishers ultimately felt that a more implied style would still be more suitable for sales and public displays of those books and therefore stuck to a nipple-free policy for the rest of the series.

Ironically though this may therefore be Malko's most risqué cover, in the book itself he gets less nookie than in other books of the series. His female partner makes it painfully obvious to him that she is expecting professional behavior from him but has no qualms about letting him watch her seduce one of the henchmen on the beach to draw attention away from Malko and allow him to do some research.

Especially at the beginning and end of the novel there is indeed a genuine sense of loss and the risks to be taken during such a mission together with the expected mélange of sex, intrigue, and violence.

And, as usual with these books, we even get some interesting factoids thrown at us: When I learnt that Eric Gairy, Grenada's first Prime Minister, was a self-proclaimed UFO nut who even lectured the UN about this topic I did a double take over this kind of Fortean

"See, I am telling you: Behind the exploitation elements these books are very educational indeed."

outrageousness but further research indeed revealed this to be true.

See, I am telling you: Behind the exploitation elements these books are very educational indeed.

Malko 62 - Bitter Snow from Puerto Rico

Bitterer Schnee aus Puerto Rico was published as Malko #62 in Germany. It was #69 of the French series where it is known as **LE TUEUR DE MIAMI (The Killer of Miami)**. The action takes place in 1983 and Vice president George H.W. Bush is actually name dropped a few times as one of the decision makers in question.

The CIA gets wind of a major drug/weapons deal with Cuba worth $50 Million and sends Malko to capture Miguel Cuevas, the notorious "Cocaine Cowboy" and drug overlord who has organised the deal, before it can take place. Cuevas is a follower of the Santería Cult, the Cuban religion similar to Voodoo, and is ready to upgrade from animal sacrifices to human victims.

Apart from a brief initial sequence in Puerto Rico and a blazing finale around islands off the coast of Cuba, the majority of the story is set in Miami, making this a somewhat less "exotic" affair than other novels in the series. The locations feel more familiar whereas often half the fun of reading the books is genuinely learning something new about history or politics of regions that are generally less well known or accessible to Western readers.

In contrast to most other novels in this series this is also less spy and espionage based but more of a conventional war on drugs men's adventure.

That is, conventional yes but with a typical smattering of sex and violence.

The novel begins with the brutal interrogation of a CIA informer. Having burnt out most of his vision via acidic eye drops, Cuevas performs sex with a local lass in front of the informer. The problem: as sex obsessed as he is, years of using cocaine made Cuevas impotent and when the girl fails to properly make him perform, he just kills her off before again focusing on the informer.

Sex in front of potential victims to demonstrate his virility is his forte which leads Malko at a later stage to mock him that the girl must have clearly been faking it.

Malko himself of course fairs much better with the ladies even though some of his conquests appear questionable in the modern era: one particular female detective (and fiancée of Malko's contact in the police force) falls asleep in a car next to him while on a lookout and in some kind of sleep induced trance pleasures him orally which he graciously accepts without hesitation. Lucky for him and for possible woke readers of the future, she then "awakes" with a laugh. She was of course a total nympho and had to pretend she was not in control.

The action pieces are fast and furious. The obvious way to do research is by introducing undercover cops as hookers into the Miami club world. Not everyone of the good guys makes it out alive and De Villiers has a habit of making us care for the characters (especially the females ones) enough that their demise leaves something of a melancholic loss.

Malko is threatened to become Cueva's first human sacrifice on the advice of the drug lord's personal Santería priest and personal advisor who tells him that burying goats alive simply will no longer do. That guy is wheelchair bound and only rats out his boss when he is threatened to be thrown into oncoming highway traffic. And when he does, the agent in charge does accidentally let him slip from his fingers after all, ensuring a suitably brutal ending for that guy.

Ooops.....

Malko 66 - Countdown to Death in Surinam

The German Malko #66 **COUNTDOWN DES TODES IN SURINAM (Countdown to Death in Surinam)** is a translation of the French SAS 71 **AVENTURE AU SURINAM (Adventure in Surinam)**, first published in 1983.

The Dutch Government is looking for an experienced madman willing to infiltrate Surinam, their former colony, and rescue an eminence grise of the current regime who has fallen foul of the dictator and been sentenced to death.

While also robbing a bank of millions in gold bullion.

With no official support other than those of a Dirty Dozen style of local killers and cutthroats.

Malko agrees. Hell ensues.

Apart from the usual mix of foreign espionage, sex and action, there are two main points that will stay in mind.

First we learn a good bit about what motivates Malko. When he is offered a sure fire suicide mission as a special favour to a friend and for no pay as the budget doesn't spread that far, he reasons that he can always refuse a paid assignment but never a request from a friend. But even though he is happy to work without remuneration for once, he wants word to spread that he was generously rewarded... especially when it comes to his fiancée Alexandra.

Next we, and that is: I, learn a lot about Surinam's political and local atmosphere and culture at the time. Though Dutch seems the official language, a lot of the characters speak Taki-Taki, an English/Dutch/Chinese influenced Creole dialect. "Bruine bonen" (brown beans) appears to be a popular Surinamese dish. Even the street descriptions for Paramaribo as well as those of small villages in the middle of nowhere sound correct. (Believe me, I did some random checks on Google Maps and was surprised how accurate a lot of the info was.)

"It bears reminding that those earlier novels were written in a time pre-internet and those little bits of local flavour would not have been easy to come by."

It bears reminding that those earlier novels were written in a time pre-internet and those little bits of local flavour would not have been easy to come by so no doubt De Villiers either relied on personal experience or on information provided by others.

And of course I am ignorant enough that the name Dési Bouterse, the military coup leader from 1980 and subsequent longterm president, meant nothing to me at all.

It is Bouterse's former friend and confidant Julius Harb that Malko is sent to save from the death sentence and fly out to Holland. The planning and execution of this affair makes this very much a heist thriller with the added suspense that, with the exception of some of the female characters (each and every one of them a nymphomanic), none of Malko's crew is reliable and all of them are just focused on how they can keep the gold for themselves and get rid of Harb.

Malko's main conspirator and ultimately antagonist is Herbert Van Mook, a shady pimp and brutal killer with good connections to the underworld who is able to organise a team of mercenaries and runs a dealership of exotic animals. One of those, an anaconda, on occasion serves as a love toy for his girlfriend Rachel. Another one, a rattlesnake, is used as a weapon against Malko in the later stages of the operation.

The team is faced with multiple set backs. The execution is put forward; airplane landing strips have become inoperable; government curfews make communication and reconnaissance difficult.

In a further look into Malko's character we see him leave Van Mook behind in a jungle with his share of the promised gold as a reward even though he had tried killing him. Of course someone like Van Mook is never happy with nearly getting away with murder so we do ultimately get a more satisfactory showdown after all.

Oh, and of course the Cubans are again mentioned as the main supporters of the Surinamese uprising. De Villiers sure had it in for them. Has there ever been an **SAS Malko** novel without at least a cursory mention of them?

Malko 75 - The Widow of the Ayatollah

The German Malko #75 **DIE WITWE DES AYATOLLAH** (**The Widow of the Ayatollah**) is a translation of the French SAS 78 **LA VEUVE DE L'AYATOLLAH** (same translation as the German title), first published in 1985.

The more I recently read Malko again the more I became intrigued not just about how easily translations are (or are not) available in different languages and how this impacts the international awareness of certain cultural icons but also about the reputation this series has in general.

It has often been described as sleazy or downright pornographic though neither the German nor the English versions I have read would warrant this extreme description.

True, they all feature generous dollops of sexual escapades and even on occasion questionable attitudes to rape or consent but all in all they do come across as comparatively tame with a larger focus on the espionage or action scenes which leads me to suspect that both translations may have been sanitised to appeal to the readers of the new target markets.

What I ultimately would love to see is an article comparing all the different translations with their source novel to see what (if anything) was amended. Unfortunately my own French language skills are too rudimentary to even contemplate this kind of venture but I sincerely hope someone else more fluent in all three languages could come to the rescue.

There are two very obvious examples in this novel where I suspect entire scenes may have been cut:

One sees Malko in New York arranging a hook up with an old flame just to then be told he'd need to board a plane for his new mission right away and say Adieu to his planned date. In a later scene he meets two girls in Marbella who bring him to a house where it appears that an orgy is just about to start. Malko, however, takes the keys to a car and heads back to his hotel.

What purpose would there be to tease the reader (in a series with a certain notoriety!) with hints of sexy time, just to then pull back from those?

Still, the book runs at 191 pages so is not exactly thin for a men's adventure type novel. And yes, it does still feature sufficient bedroom (and beach and yachting and...) action next to the more traditional Secret Agent stuff.

Malko sure does a lot of globetrotting here. The bulk of the novel is set in the British Virgin Islands but we also see him show up in New York where the likes of Andy Warhol and Grace Jones have small cameos, Switzerland, Vienna and the Costa de Sol.

He is sent to look after the Indian widow of an Ayatollah who is in possession of important secret documents and her husband's ill-gained fortune and as such is being chased by both the US and Iranian secret service.

The widow is reputedly so rich that when her ash tray is full, she throws away her Rolls Royce! She is also man hungry and a) first makes love to Malko only after he slaps her when she accuses him of being just after her money and b) subsequently threatens him with a gun and demands he'll love her or she'll kill him. No wonder he quickly becomes so infatuated with her that in order to protect her, he rejects CIA instructions and temporarily gets fired, leaving his castle potentially forever in a state of disrepair.

As usual, parts of the De Villiers' research had me hit Google. His description of the Savak, the Shah's intelligence service, and Khomeini's successor organisation as well as details about the British involvement in the Ayatollah's rise to power, all at least appear very realistic for someone as ignorant as me about the inner workings of the Iranian revolution.

Mandy Brown, a recurring character in the novels, also makes some memorable appearances in this book. All one needs to know about her is that in the French books she is known as "*Mandy la salope" (Mandy, the slut).*

For more of Holger's writing, check out his e-books **The Many Masks of Dr. Mabuse** and **Ollie's Last Round** which are available through Amazon.

DAVID 'THE PREACHER' WILSON CHATS TO LEE GOLDBERG AND JOEL GOLDMAN OF BRASH BOOKS AND CUTTING EDGE BOOKS

A BRASH ENDEAVOUR

Author's Note: I first became aware of Lee Goldberg when I discovered his wonderful books based on the popular television series **Monk**. Imagine my surprise when I discovered that Lee Goldberg has done much more than simply write books based on television programs. In fact, Lee has both written and produced television programs. His encyclopedic volume of **Unsold Television Pilots 1955-1989** is an interesting description of television history that was not to be. He has written a number of bestselling novels as well.

He continues to be active in writing fiction and his bestselling novel **Lost Hills** marked a grand entrance into realistic police procedurals that are every bit as good as Michael Connelly's **Harry Bosch** series. When he is not writing bestsellers or overseeing television production he works as the publisher of Brash books, which primarily publishes old gems of little-known or forgotten authors.

"We don't want potential readers to dismiss these stories as antiques from their grandfather's library. The goal is to draw a new generation of readers to these books."

David: How did you get into publishing?

Lee: This happened by, well, happenstance. All mystery writers have them – the cherished, often under-appreciated, out-of-print books that we loved and that shaped us as writers. They are the books that made an impression on me in my teenage and college years and still feel new and vital to me today. They are the books that I talk about to friends, thrust into the hands of aspiring writers, and that I wish I'd written. They are the yellowed, forgotten paperbacks I keep buying out of pure devotion whenever I see them in used bookstore--even though I have more copies than I'll ever need. I've been at this long enough that many of my own books have fallen out-of-print, too. But I brought them back in new, self-published Kindle and paperback editions and, to my surprise and delight, they sold extremely well. It occurred to me that if I could do it for my books, why couldn't I do the same thing for all those forgotten books that I love.

A little over six years ago, I started negotiating with the estate of an author (Ralph Dennis) whose books I greatly admired. Those books had sadly never achieved the wide readership and acclaim that they deserved. I was in the midst of those talks when, at a Bouchercon in Albany, I told my buddy Joel Goldman, a good friend, mystery writer, lawyer, and a successful self-publisher of his own backlist,

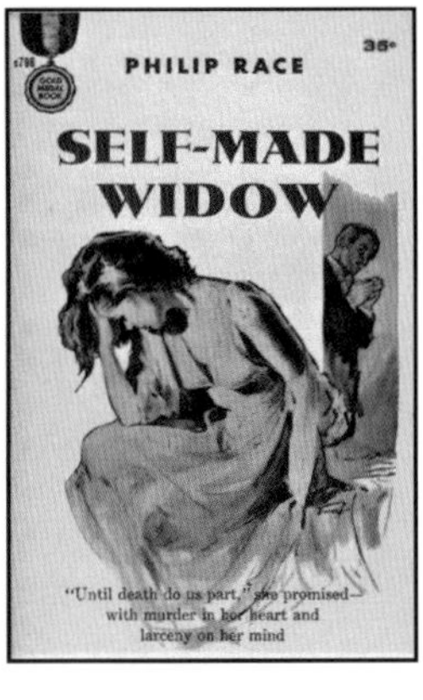

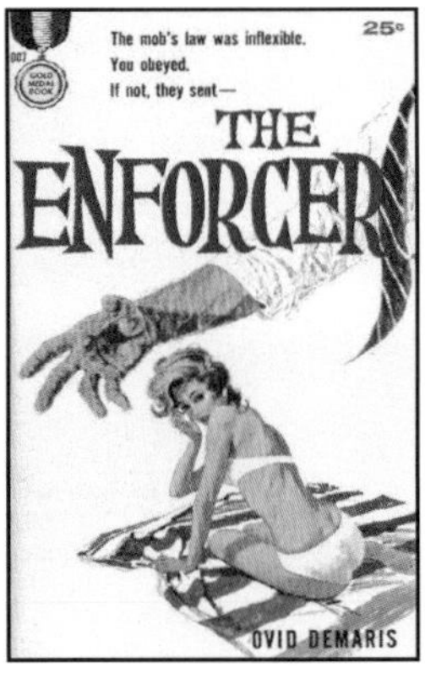

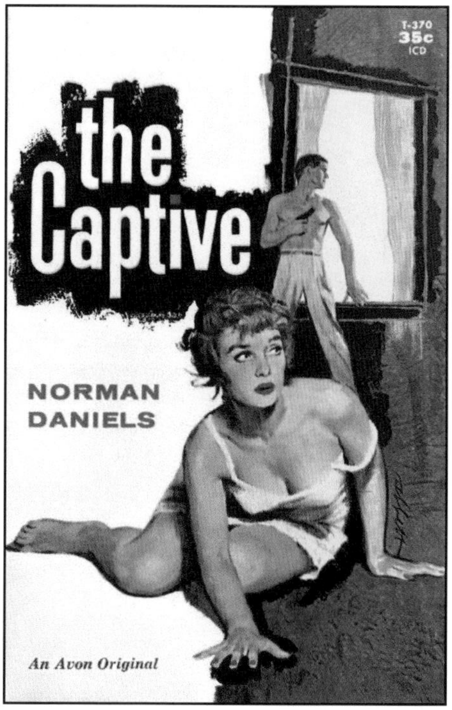

"They are the books that I talk about to friends, thrust into the hands of aspiring writers, and that I wish I'd written. They are the yellowed, forgotten paperbacks I keep buying out of pure devotion whenever I see them in used bookstores."

what I had in mind. Joel got this funny look on his face and said, "That's a business model. I really think we're really on to something. We could really make this work." We?

It turned out that, like me, he'd been getting hit up constantly at that conference by author-friends who were desperate for his advice on how they could replicate his self-publishing success with their own out-of-print books. Many of these books had won wide acclaim and even the biggest awards in our genre. Joel had been trying to think of a way he could help them out. Now he thought he had the solution: What if we combined the two ideas? What if we republished the books that we had loved for years as well as the truly exceptional books that only recently fell out of print? It sounded great to me. And at that moment, without any prior intent, we became publishers of what we considered to be the best crime novels in existence. It was a brash act, and that's how, as naturally as we became publishers, we found our company name. Brash Books.

David: How difficult is it to obtain the rights to the materials you publish?

Lee: It has been easy at times and other times it has been extremely difficult and expensive. The easy cases have been reaching out to authors I know personally or who are friends of authors I know personally. It gets hard when the author is a stranger, or has disappeared, or wrote under a pseudonym, or moved to another country, or has died. We have frequently been forced to employ a private detective to hunt down authors, estates, and to sort out who actually has the rights to some of the out-of-print books we've wanted to acquire. It was a real odyssey acquiring the rights to the Ralph Dennis books and searching for his lost manuscripts. I have written about this journey in several essays for **CrimeReads** and my quest was even covered by **Publishers Weekly**.

David: Can you tell me about how these people have been impacted by your work?

Lee: The widows and families of some of the dead authors we've republished have been delighted by the royalties, but I believe they are even more delighted just seeing the books brought lovingly and respectfully back into print to reach a new audience. I've had the widows and children of dead authors call me up in tears upon receiving the new copies of the books. They are often joyful to simply see them back in print and sad that the authors didn't live to see their books finally released so beautifully. I have to say I often end up in tears, too, when I get those calls.

Joel: I'm most proud of bringing back Barbara Neely's series featuring Blanche White. Barbara was a ground-breaking author who blazed a trail for women and minority crime writers. We were thrilled when the Mystery Writers of America named her a Grand Master in 2019. While she was able to enjoy the honour, she passed away shortly before the awards banquet.

Lee: In other cases, like Ralph Dennis and Carolyn Weston, I have bought the copyrights outright from the authors estates-- meaning

"I was at a crime writers conference somewhere, standing in the book room, when author Bill Crider, an old friend of mine, approached me with a tattered, paperback copy of a Hardman novel in his hand. He insisted that I buy it."

that I am, for all intents and purposes, I am now Ralph Dennis and Carolyn Westin in terms of their literary lives. I am not paying royalties to anybody on books that I've republished that have fallen into the public domain, because by definition they now belong to everybody. There is nothing I can do to prevent another, or ten other, or fifty other publishers from releasing the same book. That said, I am not, like so many other publishers who reissue PD work, using the original covers because the art work has not fallen into public domain, the rights belong to the artists or their estates or to the publishers (or whoever has acquired or been assigned the companies rights/assets). There are many publishers who use the original artwork anyway, despite violating the copyright (and moral rights) of the artists because they believe it's a low-risk proposition. What are the odds of being sued?

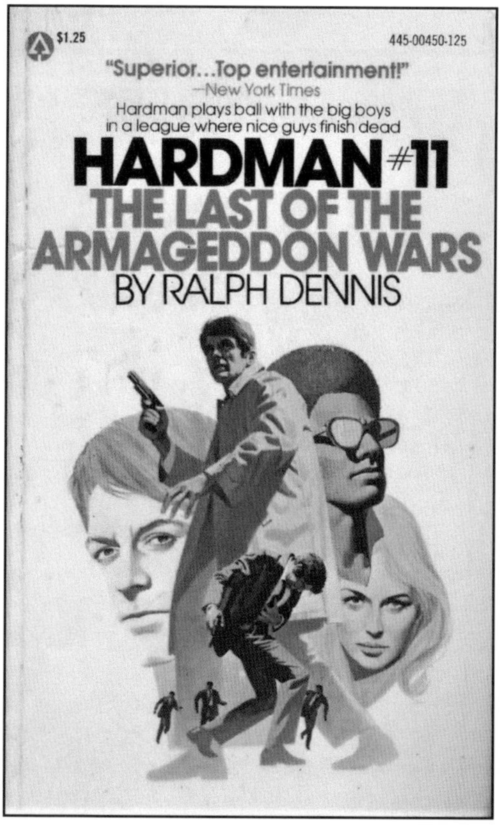

And even if you are, odds are you can get away with just dropping the cover and adding a new one. I won't play that game out of respect to the artists.

In those cases where copyright to an out-of-print work hasn't expired, finding the author or whomever owns the rights now is not impossible, but it can be very time consuming and expensive. There are sleazy publishers out there who are too cheap and too unscrupulous to go to the cost and trouble, again believing that the odds of getting caught or sued are small. I won't do that. We have spent tens of thousands of dollars on private eyes and lawyers to not only find the legitimate rights holders, but to make certain they actually do hold the rights they think or claim they have. In one case, we found the widow of an author, and she believed she had the rights to her dead spouse's work, but unbeknownst to her, she didn't. The rights had been bequeathed to, and shared by three institutions (a library, a hospice and a performing arts center). The three institutions have been unable to agree to any deal with anyone, so this author's books have remained out of print. Another author's books were willed to his wife, when she died to her sister, and when she died to her four children. All four children must agree to a deal (and not one of them had ever met the author!) In that case, one child refuses to make a deal, so the books have remained out of print, though we keep going back to them to see if she has changed her mind.

David: You mentioned the quest to gain the rights to the Hardman material?

Lee: I was at a crime writers conference somewhere, standing in the book room, when author Bill Crider, an old friend of mine, approached me with a tattered, paperback copy of a Ralph Dennis Hardman novel in his hand. He insisted that I buy it.

It was obvious from the numbered title that it was one of those cheap, men's action adventure paperbacks, a genre I knew well, having written, under the pseudonym "Ian Ludlow," a series called .357 Vigilante in the mid-1980s. While there were some gems in the genre, as readers of **Men of Violence** well know, most of them were hack work, badly written excuses for explicit sex and graphic violence that were sold in grocery store spinner racks nationwide. And a book called "Hardman"—wink, wink, nudge nudge—promised to be among the worst of them.

Bill must have seen the skepticism on my face so he smiled and said, "Trust me. You won't regret it." He was a kind, decent, warm man, an acclaimed author, and an expert on crime fiction. So I took his word for it and bought the book and quickly read it. I loved it. I immediately devoured all 12 **Hardman** novels, which I freaking LOVED, then I read Ralph's three other published novels. They were good, but they weren't the same as **Hardman**, and in the case of **MacTaggart's War**, what I saw most was the squandered potential, a book that might have succeeded if only he'd had a good editor. It was frustrating. I wished there was something I could do about it and some way I could get **Hardman** out to a wider audience. And then it hit me—maybe I could. I'd enjoyed a lot of success self-publishing my out-of-print backlist, in some cases making much more money off the new editions of my books than I did when they were originally released. I figured if I could do it for my own work, why couldn't I do it for Ralph?

I did some digging and learned the rights to Ralph's books had passed to his sister Irma and then, upon her death, to her four heirs. Irma's attorney was kind enough to share with me Ralph's unpublished manuscripts. None of them was a lost **Hardman**, much to my disappointment, but they had potential if I could do some editorial work on them. So we launched Brash Books, and I made my pitch to Ralph's four heirs: I wanted to acquire the copyright to **Hardman** novels, and everything else that Ralph wrote, published and unpublished, and bring them back into print. I wanted the copyright, rather than simply licensing them to republish, so I would have the freedom to make the editorial changes that I felt were necessary to get his unpublished books into shape. I also wanted to significantly revise **MacTaggart's War**.

But I couldn't nail down a deal. It took three years and in the interim, we published dozens of other novels. I won't get into all the complications, but once I finally secured the rights to Ralph's work, we republished all twelve of the **Hardman** novels (with new introductions from authors like Joe R. Lansdale and Paul Bishop), his three standalone novels (**The War Heist** (aka **MacTaggart's War**), **The Broken Fixer** (aka **Atlanta**) and **A Talent for Killing** (aka **Dead Man's Game**) and some of his previously unpublished work (like **The Spy in a Box** and **Dust in the Heart**). The reviews from **Publishers Weekly**, **Mystery Scene**, **Kirkus Reviews** and many other respected critics for the reprints and new books were wildly enthusiastic. The only sad thing was that Ralph wasn't alive to see it.

All of the time I spent editing Ralph's work made me eager to learn more about him as a person. I knew Ralph was a student, and later an instructor, at the University of North Carolina at Chapel Hill during the 1960s. So, in the summer of 2019, I went to Chapel Hill to read through Ralph's papers at the UNC library, to meet some of his old drinking buddies, and to see the places mentioned in his books.

On the flight to North Carolina, I began reading Ralph's unpublished manuscript **The Polish Wife**. It was about a disbarred lawyer-turned-Atlanta lobbyist who gets hired by a

"Men's action adventure paperbacks, a genre I knew well, having written, under the pseudonym Ian Ludlow."

"In the case of MacTaggart's War, what I saw most was the squandered potential, a book that might have succeeded if only he'd had a good editor."

lawyer to go to London to find a missing man. I immediately noticed some striking similarities between **The Polish Wife** and a **Hardman** novel. First off, **The Polish Wife** was written in what was unmistakably Hardman's first-person voice. Or was this just Ralph's voice? Additionally, the lawyer had the same name as a lawyer who had appeared in the final **Hardman** novel. That left me puzzling over the big question: Was **The Polish Wife** actually a rewrite of an abandoned **Hardman** novel? Even if it wasn't, would I be going too far, and taking too many creative liberties, if I revised it into a **Hardman** novel anyway? I certainly now had the legal right, but should I do it just because I could?

The question was eventually answered for me by Ralph himself in a letter I found in his papers in the Chapel Hill Library. It was a letter he wrote from London, where he was doing research for **MacTaggart's War**, to a professor on campus. In the letter, he wrote:

"I may do a Hardman in London for some extra money. I can do it while I'm doing the research for the real project."

It was soon followed by another letter to Wallace, dated January 10, 1977, that said this, among other things:

"If I can find a typewriter, I might write a quick Hardman in London and put that money aside for a trip to Italy and France after I've finished the big book. I can probably write the Hardman during the later afternoon hours after I return from research."

The letters were "the smoking gun" I needed to justify to myself revising **The Polish Wife** back into a Hardman novel. So that's what I did, releasing **All Kinds of Ugly** in February 2020, a long-lost, final **Hardman** novel. I can't tell you how happy that made me.

For Cutting Edge, many of our titles are already in the public domain. In those cases, there's no need to get permission from anyone, though I have had to use our private investigator a few times to double check the rights on some books to be sure they truly are out of copyright. But we've also licensed and acquired rights to books for Cutting Edge with authors and estates and we are also publishing some never-before-published "lost" novels by authors of vintage paperbacks and even some original "new" novels that don't quite fit into the Brash niche. For one thing, we aren't limited to crime novels at Cutting Edge, though most of the titles are in that genre. We are also publishing westerns, literary fiction, vintage "sleaze" fiction, and even some non-fiction.

David: Which of the Cutting Edge titles would you classify as your greatest achievement for this line?

Lee: We brought back Carolyn Weston & Jan Huckins' **Face of My Assassin**, a 1959 literary novel about racial strife in the deep south, that is like a cross between **To Kill a Mockingbird** and **In the Heat of the Night** but it predated both of them. The book got incredible reviews in its day, but fell out of print and into oblivion...and yet, sadly, it's every bit as

"I just loved Bud Clifton's tightly plotted hit-man novel The Murder Specialist, Chalmers Green's wickedly subversive, unpredictable hard-boiled gem The Scarlet Venus, and the brutal, bizarre, and totally unhinged plotting of Ledru Baker Jr.'s Brute Madness"

powerful and relevant now as it was when it first came out over sixty years ago.

I'm also delighted to have resurrected some forgotten, obscure, true masterpieces of noir by some authors nobody has heard of...

I just loved Bud Clifton's tightly plotted hitman novel **The Murder Specialist**, Chalmer Green's wickedly subversive, unpredictable hard-boiled gem The Scarlet Venus and the brutal, bizarre, and totally unhinged plotting of Ledru Baker Jr.'s **Brute Madness** (though it features some of the worst sex scenes ever written which, in their own hilariously bad way, are a guilty pleasure).

We've also dug up some long-lost Ralph Dennis short stories, in a collection called **Tales of a Sad, Fat Wordman**, that are remarkably revealing about the sad life and troubled personality of the man behind the **Hardman** novels.

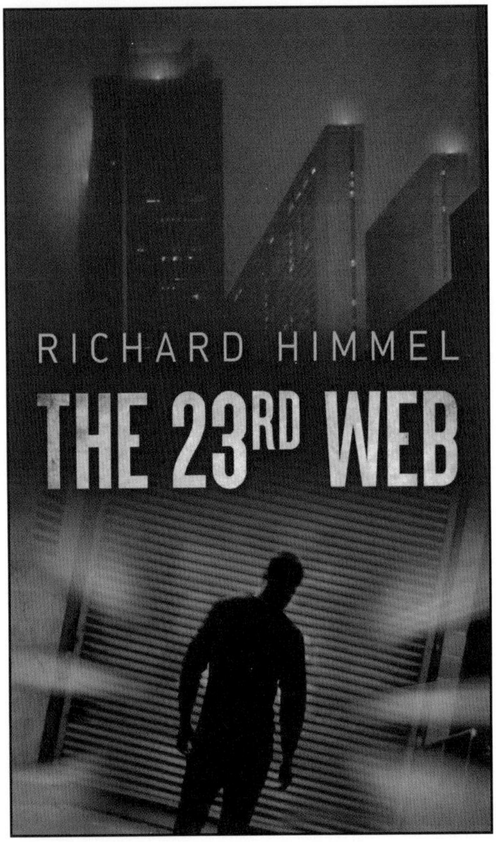

David: Can you expand on why you use utilize modern artwork rather than a vintage style?

Lee: As I mentioned earlier, while most of the books republished by Cutting Edge are in the public domain, the artwork is not. We respect copyright and we refuse to use art that we don't own. Frankly, the cost of finding whoever owns the artwork now and licensing it is prohibitively expensive. And commissioning new artwork in the same style would also be far too expensive. The profit margins on these books are slim to non-existent as it is, especially when considering that anybody can release the same public domain books that I have.

But there's also another reason we don't use vintage, or vintage-style, covers on these books. While I LOVE the old artwork, as much as I know you and your readers do, it dates the books and dooms them to appeal to a very narrow niche of

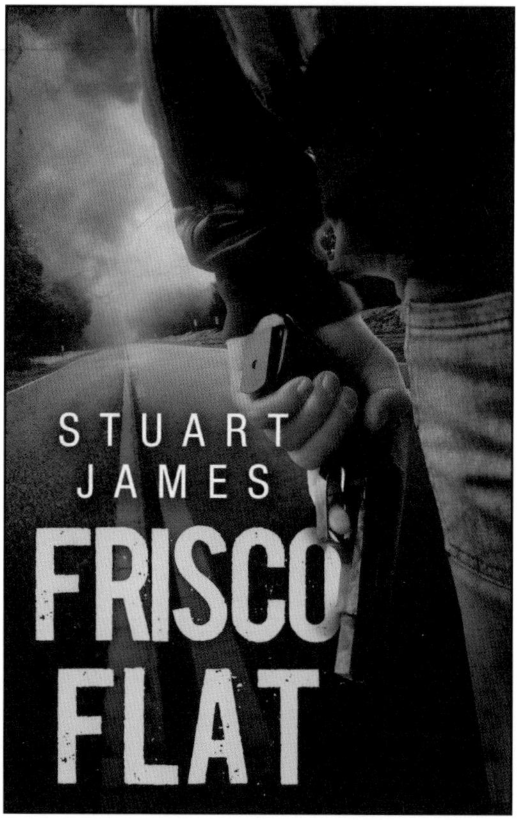

readers. We need to reach a much wider audience than that if we are going to recoup our investment in Cutting Edge and make some money, too. This is a labour of love, but it's also a business.

I'm a writer myself, and what I love about these books are stories and the writing. I buy them for that, not the covers. So that's what we're selling: the stories and the writing, not the covers. I believe that's what truly endures.

Joel: Crime fiction is not time bound. A book's appeal doesn't depend on when it was written. We choose modern artwork because we're introducing authors to new audiences and we want the books to have a fresh, contemporary appeal.

Lee: We don't want potential readers to dismiss these stories as antiques from their grandfather's library. The goal is to draw a new generation of readers to these books. We want them to fall in love with the work of these authors the way we have. We strongly believe to do that, we need the books to look new and fresh. We want to pitch these as compelling crime stories that just happen to be written in and set in the past. We believe that they are as relevant, entertaining and satisfying as any crime novels set in present day or as any new books written and published today that happen to be set in the past. Packaging them as "vintage" work will push away the new readers we want to attract.

The success of our reprints at Brash proved that strategy works so that's the approach we've taken with Cutting Edge as well.

David: How do you choose the materials you seek to "republish?

Lee: First, as I mentioned before, it began with a list of books that I loved. The late Bill Crider also recommended a lot of great books to us. For Cutting Edge, our new vintage books imprint, I've received terrific advice from the team at Paperback Warrior and from the posts on the 'Men's Adventure Paperbacks of the 20th Century' Facebook Group. I've discovered a lot of titles on my own at used bookstores and vintage paperback shows.

David: Lee and Joel, thanks for chatting to me and all the best for 2021.

JUSTIN MARRIOTT ON THE RENEGADE PUBLISHING HOUSE, MANOR BOOKS

GRINDHOUSE PUBLISHING

Manor Books were the New York based publisher whose catalogue, packaging and business tactics were reminiscent of the exploitation films that played at the grindhouses in the notorious 42nd Street district. As you will probably be aware, the exploitation movies copied popular themes from films produced by mainstream studios and produced their own low-budget versions, with added sex and violence to compensate for a lack of production values and name actors. The grindhouse theatres that showed these exploitation movies had little regard to the quality of the movies they showed, with their focus being on quantity as their modus operandi were triple-bills and 24 hours opening. Kung-fu, cannibal and chicks-in-chains were all popular genres in the grindhouses.

Manor operated at even lower level on the publishing ladder than Pinnacle or Belmont Tower, and applied the exploitation movie techniques to their output. Pinnacle may have invented the men's adventure series with the likes of **The Executioner**, but Mack Bolan wouldn't have knocked a nun out cold with a sucker punch (**Mondo**), used spiked knuckle-dusters (**Gannon**), encountered an ex-Vietnam veteran with a taste for human flesh (**Keller The Cannibal**) or featured a castrated criminal who commands a giant praying mantis to rip the breasts off women in his quest for vengeance (**Eat Them Alive**).

It wasn't just the contents of Manor Books which were rough. Another distinctive characteristic of Manor's publications are the way their covers have physically worn. Many of the second-hand copies I've picked up have covers scarred with strange scuff marks which I've not observed on any other used-book. Not all their paperbacks have physically aged in such a bizarre manner, but presumably at some point the company employed a cheap(er) printing process which means the paper and card have deteriorated more noticeably than other books of that period.

Their business practices were rumoured to be rough as well. Manor once published a SF book called **Titans of the Universe** by James Harvey, which was copyrighted to 'Moonchild' and later found to be a word-for-word copy of an earlier Gardner Fox effort **Escape from Cosmos**.

They had a hardcore porn fiction line Pleasure Books, which pirated other titles and often reprinted the same story under different titles, sometimes in the same batch of releases, presumably without paying the author.

Jack Moskovitz wrote a book called **The Arson Job** as Jack Moss for them, and later quipped in an interview published in **Books Are Everything** fanzine that, "Manor had no manners." In a memoir from Stephen Mertz (page 44), other authors that were on the wrong end of Manor are mentioned.

Initially the packaging of Manor Boooks was professional and eye-catching, with cover art from professionals such as Ken Barr, Bob Larkin, Bruce Minney, George Gross and Raymond Kursar.

But I wonder if there was a change in ownership, as later in the Manor run, the covers were often reuses of existing art, sometimes recycled from previous Manor Books even if their relevance to the content is tenuous at best, or badly-reproduced and washed-out images from UK paperbacks, a tactic most seen on their SF paperbacks with Bruce Pennington the artist most likely to be pirated.

Also the lettering began to resemble letraset transfers - the type I used to use on fanzines in the 1980s - and at times weren't even in a straight line.

For a period in the mid-1970s they carried the Manor Books "Seal of guaranteed READER satisfaction. If you purchase any Manor Book with the above seal and you decide you were disappointed in any way, simply return the book to the publisher with only 25c to cover postage and handling." I suspect I know how Manor would respond to any reader foolhardy enough to take them up on the offer.

MANOR BOOKS 12333 ★
MONDO
ANTHONY DE STEFANO
He did you a favor–
if you died fast.

MANOR BOOKS
MEET GANNON:
#1
He's after vengeance...and leaves behind a trail of blood and gore.
Blood For Breakfast
DEAN BALLENGER

MANOR BOOKS 12270 ★ $1.25
THE BRUTALLY AUTHENTIC NEW SERIES
KELLER
NELSON DE MILLE
THE CANNIBAL
A cannibal was terrorizing the city, and Det. Sgt. Keller was hungry for the kill.

EAT THEM ALIVE
PIERCE NACE
HIS THIRST FOR REVENGE WAS UNQUENCHABLE UNTIL HE STUMBLED ON THE TERRIFYING MONSTERS OF MALPELO ISLAND
FIRST TIME IN PAPERBACK

Little is documented about Manor, but the rumours run thick and fast. I will start with the facts, as best I know, then move into the speculation and intrigue. Manor Books was incorporated in December 1971 by Walter Weidenbaum, a lawyer by trade who got into the publishing business. Weidenbaum had been involved in Pinnacle Books, possibly also Bee Line, the sleaze publishing imprint that launched Pinnacle. I think the trigger for the formation of Manor was the decision by MacFadden-Bartell to exit the paperback business, and offering their back catalogue for sale.

Manor Books stopped issuing new books in 1981, and closed in June 1993. The company changed its name three times, which seemed commonplace with lower-rung publishers of the time. In 1971 it was Smash Enterprises, in early 1972 it was America Affairs Press and in mid-72, became Manor Books, Inc.

Other names associated with Manor Books include Morris Weintraub (better known as Murray Traub), Henry McQueeney and Anthony DeStefano. McQueeney was described as a tough-guy editor that you would not tangle with. DeStefano's name would appear as cover designer and author, as well as taking editorial duties.

There were rumours that Manor were Mafia owned, but I have never seen this substantiated. It is known that the Mafia controlled large sections of book and magazine distribution, as well as porn shops, so any lower rung publisher would inevitably rub against organised crime. One author who wrote for Belmont Tower/Leisure and Manor, has speculated they were all one company. I can't see the connection in terms of the physical books, but the 70s publishing world could be a shady one.

On the whole, the Manor catalogue was mediocre and lowest common denominator. However, if you lock in to that grindhouse mentality, there are a number of titles/series which do offer guilty pleasures, although on-line sellers are charging accordingly. Over the following pages I'll present a gallery of Manor paperbacks which fall into the men's adventure and thriller categories.

Part of the short-lived (thankfully) trucker-exploitation genre created by the success of the Convoy movie. The frontispiece states "Sci-Fi Greats" which says it all about Manor's approach to detail and quality.

Author Feinman specialised in non-fiction 'How Tos', and this was a rare excursion into fiction. He may be a Feinman, but fine author he is not. The film never appeared, which may well have been a bogus claim from Manor.

A bridge between Block's earlier pseudonymous, sleaze paperbacks and his more crafted crime fiction. Based on a friend who unexpectedly lost their job in magazine editing, Block's story is told through letters.

Charles Miron was one of Manor's most prolific authors. Because no other authors hung around at Manor for long, I wonder if Miron was a pseudonym for a member of the editorial staff.

A fizzy beverage aimed at African-Americans which makes them sterile. Told through a combination of transcripts and narrative, this is surprisingly well-written for a Manor Book. Laric had been a film scripter.

One of the few decent reads in Manor Book's 'Hawk Editions' line of war novels. The second entry to the **Glasshouse Gang** series about a group of ex-cons who live like outlaws in WW2 North Africa.

John Crowe was the pseudonym used by Denis Lynds for a Buena Costa County mystery series of 5 books. Lynds works as Mark Sadler were also reprinted by Manor. This was the only Crowe that Manor repackaged.

All of the lower-rung publishers issued a paperback featuring snuff movies, as the theory of their existence spread. This is told partially from the view of the actress who relays the director's increasing demand for "realness."

Jack Cummings was actually John Cummings, who went onto success in non-fiction real estate guides. This was his only title for Manor Books, a Florida-set thriller in the world of drug-smuggling.

Another Miron Manor, this time a heist paper. I have included it because it is an example of a reused cover - originally for **The Unicorn**, the first and only (?) entry to a Psychic Detective series by Hans Holzer.

A reprint of a 1948 crime novel about the murder of two young girls and its impact upon the community, told through the eyes of those impacted, including the sixteen year-old perpetrator. A classic.

The things I do in the name in the research.... an example of one of Manor's hardcore sleaze Pleasure Books line, **Hot House** is about a sleazy landlord. I assure you there is little pleasure to be had from this book.

Movie tie-in to the film that was used **The Chase** by Richard Unekis as its springboard. Without any doubt, a superior read to 99% of the Manor product listed in these pages.

Theodore Claw is the ex-boxer and baseball pitcher whose career was ended by losing some fingers, so now works as an undercover agent busting drug-smugglers. Insert baseball pun of your choice.

Aimed at the Harold Robbins market, this an absolute-power-corrupts soap-opera about a rich family that effectively run a small-town. Yawn. Other Moore's for Manor in this vein included **Blind Spot** and **Aloha**. Less please.

The Dynamite Freaks was another of the short-lived 'Now Books for Now People' packaged up by Lyle Kenyon Engel for Manor Books, with Donald Ryan being a pseudonym. It is about a radicalised female student.

Edward Aarons had a number of his mysteries published at MacFadden books and presumably Manor picked this up when they bought elements of their catalogue. It's a nifty small town plagued by killer mystery.

A repackaging of a 1962 thriller about a double-crossed photographer caught up in a small-town scandal. The racy images and re-titling intentionally make the story appear much more racy.

Death of a City was a rare paperback edition of a later White novel, which unlike his typical heist-caper, had its roots in fact. A riot spreads from a church explosion and consumes a Southern town.

No Beast So Fierce was an edition of Edward Bunker's unrelentingly grim and gripping semi-autobiographical account of an ex-convict struggling with life outside of prison. Hoffman starred in the film adaptation.

Death Never Forgets was a soldier- of- fortune thriller featuring three super-tough French Foreign legionnaires, weaved into the actual assassination attempts made on the life of King Hassan of Morocco.

The Exterminator was a tie-in to the very successful exploitation film which made great use of New York's 42nd Street as a sleazy backdrop. Written by famed editor Pete McCurtin, the story's ending differs to the film.

Cover artists often used film stills as source material, but this Charles Bronson portrait by George Gross for **The Hard Edge** must have surely pushed the boundaries of what constituted acceptable use.

The Walled Yard was White's final novel, a hard-boiled jailbreak novel with a twist. Sal Modesto is a millionaire criminal looking to break out, but subject to multiple double-crosses from a bent screw and a snitch con.

Hollywood Detective: Garrison (1975) and follow-up **The Wolf** (1975), were interesting for their setting in the movie industry of the late 1920s, at a time when the 'talkies' were causing a revolution.

Nobody Wins, was a very early thriller from Jerry Kennealy, who is now best known for his **Nick Polo** series. Kennealy was an ex-policeman and a PI who drew on this experiences vividly for his body of work.

A riff on the **Magnum Force** vigilante cop theme. The 'Mystery Editor's Award' star appeared on many Manors, without any further explanation. The art was originally on **Dachau Treasure** by Anthony De Stefano.

Sole paperback fiction excursion from Weiss, whom I understand was an academic who specialised in the Far East. At 300-pages long and with a sleazy sheen, it is a very commercial and unrewarding Cold War thriller.

A biographical novel written by a policeman with 20 years experience, which was part of the ever-green corrupt-cop genre which gained in popularity around that time because of the **Serpico** movie doing so well.

A **Jaws** cash-in written by Nelson DeMille as Brad Matthews. Reminiscent of a series of first-person memoirs from a men's adventure magazines, this is as gloriously OTT and epic as any shark-o-phile might crave.

Rape Squad must qualify as one of the most distasteful book titles of all time. Thankfully, based on the few chapters I read, the contents aren't as offensive, with an uneasy alliance of three cops working together on the unit.

Part of a short-lived genre of women P.I.s, **Nookie** was the creation of J Conaway, who also wrote the better-known/less obscure **Jana Blake** duo at Belmont Tower. This is the sequel to **Meet Nookie**.

The Assassin - no relation to other series of that name - could have been the first instalment in a series. Its lead character is a policeman who loses everything when he is framed, so become an assassin for hire.

Dennis Lynds was such a prolific crime writer that he employed Michael Collins and Mark Sadler pen-name. This was one of six books featuring Paul Shaw a PI, and is set amongst the movers and shakers of New Jersey.

Harry Harrison was known for his blending of SF and comedy in the **Stainless Steel Rat** series, and this was his attempt with a contemporary thriller when an art expert is sent to Mexico to recover paintings stolen by Nazis.

The Cop-Killers takes the prize as the most tasteless of Manor's covers, with a pile of bloodied brain cells underneath a dead policeman's cap. It was part of a unconnected 'Now Books for Today's Readers' line.

Joseph Nathenson wrote 3 books for Manor, each in a different genre - SF, horror and this thriller. Five veterans return to Europe to visit their old stomping grounds and get caught up in a web of art-smuggling.

Readers expecting the book depicted by the cover image, might have been disappointed to find **The Giant Killer** was about a Chicano boxer. I imagine the misleading cover image was reused from another Manor Book.

A gritty and grimy police procedural which is much more hard-hitting than one might expect of a Manor crime novel. Joe Kenney of the Glorious Trash blog suggests William Crawford used the David Black by-line.

Johnny Baron is the titular cult breaker in this one-off. A professional smuggler and ex-mercenary, Baron is framed into heading up a private detective agency which is dedicated to a crusade against cults.

Men's adventure with Yankowski, a boss of an international construction crew. In this one-off, Yank takes his crew to build a road on a South American island where they encounter a local guerilla group.

There were two entries to the **Tac One** series, which was a WW2 set action/adventure, featuring a **Dirty Dozen** style crew. **Assignment Devil's Playground** was followed by **Assignment North Africa**.

The first and most outrageous of the **Bronson** trilogy, in which the anti-hero is pretty much every type of 'phobe' and 'ist' going. The illustration is by Ramond Kursar, who produced a few covers for Manor.

The third of the Bronsons, with Joseph Chadwick behind the Philip Rawls pen-name for this particular variation on **Death Wish**. Again, it's Raymond Kursar's brush strokes on the cover.

George Gross art for Manor Books reprinting of a 4-book Lancer series they obtained the rights to, and added a further 2 entries. Being Manor, they got the numbering wrong, labelling book 4 as book 6!

Brightlight was Trevor Bernard's only published book, which is surprising considering the cover's comparison of him to Hammett, Spillane and Chandler marks him out at as an author of great talent.

The third of Ralph Hayes's adventurer-archaeologist quartet for Manor Books. I think this is a great cover composition, but the figure is reminiscent of the Kursar above. I don't recognise the signature on the art.

Not much in the way of kung-fu or exploding cars in this farce set in the milieu of a sleazy publishing empire, with a series of ludicrous characters. I assume Santana Arroyo was a pseudonym.

The lead is Martin Luther, which is about as subtle as Rosenberger ever gets. The famously combustible Rosenberger and Manor Books would have made uneasy bedfellows, so little surprise there were only three.

Despite the suggestion of an Airline Investigator series, this was a one-off. Credited author Howard Harris was apparently a pseudonym for an airline pilot. I guess the pseudonym is intended to suggest Howard Hughes.

Although Nelson DeMille has apparently been happy to sign his early work which appeared under his name, I don't know if he feels the same way about this decidedly sleazy number.

Presumably the book's setting in the African country of Burundi which was beset by Civil War at the time, was the thinking behind Manor selecting a cover from a men's adventure series featuring an African-American.

Pawns was about a CIA agent caught up in events leading up to the Six-Day War between the Israelis and the Arabs. The cut-off of author Soderberg's name is reflective of my copy which looks as if the trimming was wrong.

Hawk Editions was the label Manor used on a series of mostly atrocious war stories, with Karl Meyer responsible for the majority of them. The back cover blurb is so generic, it could be placed on any war book.

THE HARD EDGE

A Visual Guide to Manor's Men's Adventure series

A look at the output of everyone's favourite low-rent publisher whose series rarely ran beyond four books, presumably because about that time, the author got fed up with not being paid for their work and moved on. Cover art included excellent work from Raymond Kursar, Bob Larkin, Ken Barr and Bruce Minney. There are many examples of Manor recycling art from book to book, irrespective of how well it suited the contents. And presumably without paying the artists for secondary uses. From a collector's perspective, the on-line prices are on the increase, especially for the **Gannon** series, the titles by Nelson De Mille and gory shlocker **Eat Them Alive**.

AIRPORT COP

Now you know why its called a Terminal

Charles Miron was one of Manor's most prolific authors, who presumably had a method for making them pay him for his books! His **Airport Cop** trilogy featured Verban, the titular officer who faced serial murderers, hijacks, prostitution rings and gangland murders at JFK airport. The last book was packaged to look like a disaster novel.

BRONSON

Any similarity to tough-guy actors is coincidental

Charles Bronson was evidently a screen icon that Manor felt their target audience would identify with, as the used him as a cover model and as inspiration for this lone-wolf trilogy. The identity of the author behind the relentlessly scuzzy first instalment is unknown, with Len Levinson and Joseph Chadwick penning the other two.

CHECK FORCE

Cold War paranoia pulp

MoV legend Ralph Hayes, riffed on cold-war paranoia in six **Check Force** adventures, in which Chane a fugitive CIA agent, and Karkov a disaffected KGB spy, team up to stand against Force III, an ultra-secret cabal dedicated to seizing world control by forcing the super-powers into nuclear war.

THE ENFORCER

Talking 'bout my regeneration

The Enforcer's first four adventures appeared at Lancer, with a regeneration at Manor Books where there were 2 new entries as well as reprints of the Lancers. Manor showed their customary lack of attention by putting the number 6 on the fourth book, and giving book 1 a new title; **Caribbean Kill**. Author Andrew Sugar's life story is fascinating.

GANNON

Blood for Breakfast, Lunch and Tea.

Notoriously ultra-violent and hard-boiled trilogy featuring blood in each of its titles. Loose-cannon **Gannon** is a modern-day Robin Hood who is hired by the down-trodden to fight back against the rich and powerful. The books' reputation is generated by the Spillane-on-steroids style narrative full of invented slang and politically incorrect dialogue.

ISRAEL COMMANDOS

As timely as today's headlines

Andrew Sugar wrote four **Israeli Commandos** novels, which alternated their lead between two such soldiers. Arab terrorists are typically featured as the villains, blowing up dams, oil refineries and miniature atomic bombs. The book's blurb focused that the series was "different" and focused on current events.

KELLER

The Big Apple bites back

Future best-seller DeMille cut his teeth working on lone-wolf cops such as **Keller** at Manor Books and **Ryker** at Leisure. Keller is an even more nihilistic and macho version of **Dirty Harry**. But the most memorable character in the Keller quartet is the Big Apple, which is detailed in all of its putrid, 1970s hell-hole glory by DeMille.

KILL SQUAD

Killing in the name of....

Kill Squad were a trio of crime-fighters made up of leader Chet Tabor, Grant Lincoln a powerful black giant committed to law and order and Maria Alvarez a dedicated Chicana cop who was not afraid to throw away the book and write her own deadly rules. They appeared in four adventures, all of which had a variation on Dead in the title.

KUNG FU

Manor are early to the kung-fu cash-in craze

Three authors and two pseudonyms contributed to the **Mace** series, which has the dubious honour to be the first of the kung-fu craze cash-ins. Joseph Rosenberger claims some form of record for the number of racist terms used in the books he penned. He also uses the phrase "nuts turned to jelly" which strikes me as something of a classic.

MONDO

Fight dirty!

A skuzzy martial-arts trilogy consisting of **Mondo**, **Cocaine Kill** and **A Minute to Pray, a Second to Die** written by Manor Books art editor De Stefano. Mondo is a bad-ass ninja hiding in a cloak of alcoholism, who is rescued by his master who is then be killed by the Mafia, sparking Mondo into a revenge mission.

MR DYNAMITE

From Germany with love

Mr Dynamit (no e) was a long-running spy character appearing in German language Heftroman magazines, who was selected for reprints in the US, initially by Pinnacle who gave up after one, then Manor who pumped out 6 reprints in 1977. The books betray their origin as factory-churned fast-fiction.

MURDER MASTER

The Death Merchant author visits Manor

Three **Murder Master** adventures appeared at Manor, about African-American PI Luther "Lou" King. Anyone familiar with the politics or books of author Joseph Rosenberger will see he is not a natural for the material. Needless to say it was over quickly and Rosenberger focused on his success with **Death Merchant** at Pinnacle Books.

OPERATION HANG TEN

Life's a beach!

One of a few series that Manor picked up from MacFadden Books when that operation closed down. This and the **Aquanauts/Tigershark** were from legendary book packager Lyle Kenyon Engel, although neither should be considered his finest hour. Unlike the **Aquanauts** though, there was only one **Hang Ten** book at Manor and no reprints.

STONER

Raiders of the Lost

'Stoner', a veteran prospector and treasure hunter whose globe-trotting exploits were detailed in **The Satan Stone**, **The Golden God**, **All That Glitters** and **King's Ransom**. Pretty dull stuff despite attempts to make the series 'topical' by including an Erich Von Daniken type character in one episode.

TIGER SHARK

Manor and the Aquanauts meets Jaws

MacFadden Books had been printing an **Aquanauts** series when they exited the book market, and Manor picked it up. They reprinted a number of the series as well as issuing new titles. To further complicate matters, they cashed in on **Jaws** by issuing some under a **Tiger Shark** banner. Manning Lee Stokes wrote many, if not all.

FROM THE MANOR TORN

Paul Bishop writes - my friend Stephen Mertz is a prolific wordslinger who always delivers thrills and solid entertainment in every novel he writes. Like me, his early short stories were published in Mike Shayne Mystery Magazine—so we are brothers under the pen. Here, is the low down and dirty story of his first novel and the evil empire known as Manor Books, as told by Stephen in the Wolfpack Publishing reprint...

It is with considerable joy that I introduce this new edition of my very first novel, a private eye thriller seeing new life in a brand new edition from Wolfpack Publishing. Herewith a few words to amuse & elucidate concerning my experience with Manor Books, the original mass market publisher of **Some Die Hard**. And you may quote me:

Back in the day, Manor Books was a low-end New York publishing house in the 1970s, operated by pack of thieving scuzzballs.

Thank you, and good night.

What's that?

You want to know more? Well, okay. Here's the story of how Manor Books tried to screw me and how I screwed them right back, via long distance no less, without spending a penny.

I wrote **Some Die Hard** in 1975 while I was living in Denver. Private eye Rock Dugan's first and only case. I dedicated the book to my mentor and brother writer, the late Don Pendleton, who was generous and helpful in his critique of the novel in manuscript form.

Writing the book was fun. Finding a home for it with a publisher took another four years. During those four years, I sold a handful of stories to **Mike Shayne Mystery Magazine** while a New York agent circulated **Some Die Hard** for publication consideration. It received a polite round of encouraging words, but no acceptance.

"Back in the day, Manor Books was a low-end New York publishing house in the 1970s, operated by pack of thieving scuzzballs. Thank you, and good night."

After eventually quitting the agent and leaving Denver for the rural mountain life, I spotted a market report in **Writers Digest**. A mass market publisher in New York was looking for previously unpublished novelists who lived outside the New York area. The suggestion was the publisher—Manor Books by name—was reaching beyond the literary and pulp cliques of the Northeast, hunting for new talent in the heartland. Hey, that was me!

At the time, I owned a small second hand bookshop in Durango, Colorado—wall to wall unfinished wooden shelves packed with paperbacks. Actually had an entire room devoted to Harlequin romances. Until about five years earlier, Durango was strictly a cowboy and mining town. Then the hippies discovered it. The tourists came next and, by the time I arrived in the 1970s, Durango's residents grew to include people drawn from everywhere. Writers. Artists. Musicians. Movie people (parts of **Butch Cassidy & The Sundance Kid**, among other films, were shot in the area). Everyone I hung out with was from somewhere else. We preferred the back roads and the pines and peace and quiet to the city life most of us had left behind. We were young, broke

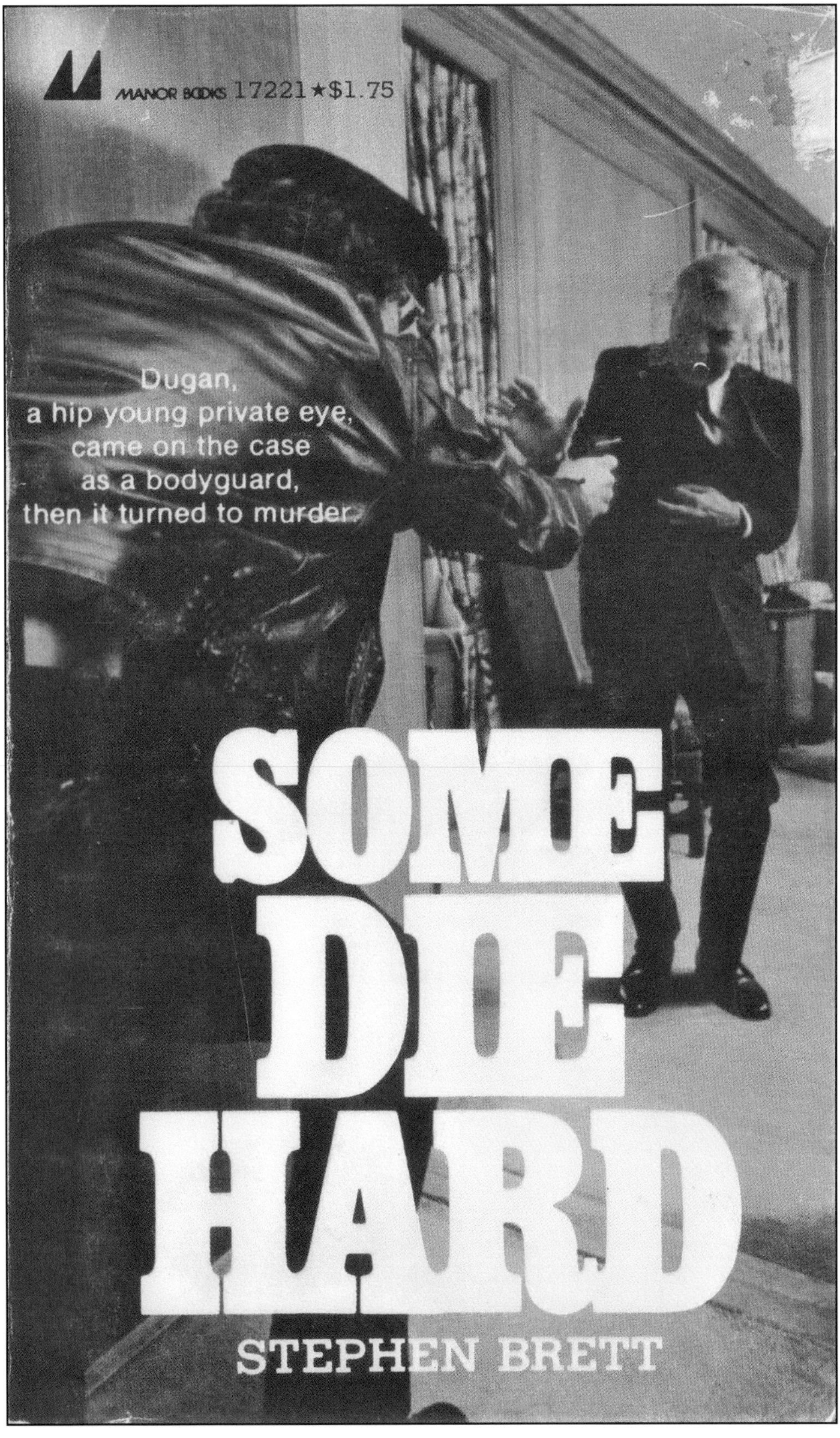
MANOR BOOKS 17221★$1.75
Dugan,
a hip young private eye,
came on the case
as a bodyguard,
then it turned to murder.
SOME DIE HARD
STEPHEN BRETT

and happy. A bohemian, hedonistic, fun lifestyle. Durango was that kind of place.

So off went **Some Die Hard**. (The novel's original title was **The Flying Corpse**, however it had been suggested a less, uh, spectacular title might stand a better chance of acceptance). Not only did I think **Some Die Hard** was a serviceable title, but so did writers Marvin H. Albert (under his Nick Quarry pseudonym) and Carroll John Daly—both of whom had used the same title in their day. I snail-mailed **Some Die Hard** over the transom (unsolicited) to Manor, and it took those slicks all of a New York minute to jump on a guy living way out in the Rockies, without a telephone.

They offered me $750.

Honestly, I was overjoyed. After four years, I felt finally vindicated as a writer. This being my first novel, though, and thinking $750 really wasn't that much money, I trudged through the snow to a neighbour's house. I asked to use their phone and called the only three published novelists I knew: Michael Avallone in New Jersey, Don Pendleton in Indiana, and Bill Pronzini in California. The unanimous advice from all three pros was to go for it. Get published. Start building a career—And ask for more money.

So I did, via a collect telephone call. Editor Larry Patterson was the soul of cordiality, promptly boosting the advance up to a thousand dollars without batting an eye. He was probably thinking, What the hell, we're not going to pay the chump anyway.

I was aware Manor Books was a bottom line concern, so I decided to use a pseudonym to avoid getting boxed in as a low-rent writer. Hence, the original penname Stephen Brett—the surname being a tribute to Brett Halliday (aka: Davis Dresser), a favorite writer of the private eye stories I'd been reading since high school. Manor moved fast. There was money to be made. Within weeks I had a contract in hand for the astronomical sum of one thousand dollars, payment due upon publication.

ONE THOUSAND DOLLARS!

Dang. Where do I sign? My writing journal indicates I had fifty-four cents to my name the day that contract arrived.

The book was printed and bound (cheaply, with a recycled cover photo from an earlier Manor title, Tether's End by Margery Allingham) and shipped. It was on sale within months, even in remote little ol' Durango (the nearest cities being Albuquerque—4 hours away—and Denver—8 hours away). Since local friends were buying my book, supposedly so were readers from coast to coast. The book was reviewed in **Ellery Queen Mystery Magazine**. The reviewer thought it was okay.

However, I hadn't gotten paid. Hmm. Okay. I'll

"...Boosting the advance up to a thousand dollars without batting an eye. He was probably thinking, What the hell, we're not going to pay the chump anyway."

call Larry. Quoth Larry, "Sorry, Steve. We're a little backed up, blah, blah, blah. The check will be in the mail by the end of the week." Great...Except the check wasn't in the mail, that week or any of the following weeks.

The months dragged on. I still didn't have a phone. Sometimes I'd pester my neighbor. Other times, if I was in town, I'd used one of the old-fashioned wooden telephone booths

MANOR EYES: Texas Wind by James Reasoner and **Some Die Hard** by Stephen Mertz

Manor Books never hit the big time. But along the way they published the first novels of James Reasoner and Stephen Mertz (writing as Stephen Brett) both are old-school private eye novels of a the highest quality. Both authors have had good careers in books with numbers on them, Mertz in the Bolan world, plus **M.I.A. Hunter** and others. Reasoner in westerns mostly with series like **Longarm** and **Trailsman.** Its clear they both love their private eyes though, both books are great tributes to the characters that came before but yet build on the concept of "one man vs. them all" that is the central theme of detective fiction and put it through the lens of their respective times and places.

Texas Wind is the best Mike Shayne novel ever written, but of course it's not it being the only novel-length appearance of Cody, a Fort Worth private investigator. I couldn't help comparing the two as Cody and Shayne are some of the best representations of the classic version of the American Private Detective out there. I think Mr. Reasoner will appreciate the Shayne reference (if he ever reads this, yeah right!) as he cut his teeth writing Shayne some of the best novelettes for **Mike Shayne Mystery Magazine** and has an affection for the character. Shayne has gotten the tag of "generic P.I." which is unfair in my opinion as Shayne lives in a clearly written world and he himself is fairly different in setting, temperament and habits then the cliched detective, that being said Shayne was ghost written and after a while the edges of his character were smoothed away. In a lot of ways Cody is a generic P.I. on the surface, a loner with an answering service, freshly bought Remington prints for his office, .38 and a sense of right and wrong. In lesser hands the book wouldn't be as FANTASTIC as it is. Cody pounds pavement, asks questions, sinks his teeth into a case about missing college student and doesn't let go. Along the way he tangles with mafioso, gets beaten, shot at and at one point has a severed finger in his glove box. Cody is Shayne with sharp edges and a breath of excited first-novel writing that is sometimes magical.

Some Die Hard is about Rock Dugan (GREAT NAME) a colorful Denver-based hip 70's detective trying to figure out a flying locked room mystery. Dugan's a right tough guy with a .44 magnum, a stuntman background and a love for books. Right after you meet Dugan he's reading a Perry Mason. I love things like in books. Influences on your sleeve. Dugan has to solve the death of a man who went up in a sailplane only to come down in it dead with a knife in his chest. Probably the only locked-sailplane mystery ever. Dugan's story has the hallmarks of a classic Gold Medal private eye paperback, crooked cops, the mob, rich evil people, etc. etc. But I got the Mike Shayne vibe from it as well. See, back in the early Shayne days when eye-patched David Dresser (it makes a cool author photo) was still writing them Shayne had the hard-boiled **Black Mask** edge to him tempered by a bit of the screwball and a bit of the "classic detection/locked-room" bit; i.e. gathering the suspects into a room at the end of the book and verbally spewing the tale of his investigation until the killer was apparent. This is a humdinger of hard-boiled tale that twists and fires on all .44 cylinders. Plus it's dedicated to Don Pendleton of **The Executioner** fame. Super side-note: Pendleton wrote an awesome P.I. series of his own about **Joe Copp**, so add those to your list too.

Both writers have spoken about how Manor was a screwy place to write for so that probably killed the chance of Cody or Dugan appearing in other books, much to my chagrin. Cody did appear in some short stories in various places (including, you guessed it, **Mike Shayne Mystery Magazine**) they were all collected in **Fort Worth Nights**, and it, along with **Texas Wind**, is readily available in paperback and ebook. Though Dugan was one-and-done, Stephen Mertz does now have a series set in the 70's about a tough-guy private eye named Kilroy that can be seen as a spiritual successor to Dugan. That's a terrific series, lean and mean detective stories that a few-and-far between these days. **Some Die Hard** and the Kilroy books are all in paperback and ebook too. So, you can have a lot of quality writing at your bloody little fingers pretty quick. The original paperback of **Texas Wind** and **Some Die Hard** are not readily available. **Texas Wind** in particular is a pricey book, I got lucky when I picked mine up from one of the massive online booksellers, I rolled the dice on a no picture Amazon listing and came up lucky. It only took like fifteen years of looking. Yeah, man I lead a life worth living.

Roy Nugen

then in the lobby of Durango's Strater Hotel. I'd think of Louis L'Amour, a local celeb of sorts since he had a summer place three miles north of town. It was known L'Amour had written some of his 1950s pulp westerns while staying at the Strater between jobs working in the area as a wrangler for what were then called dude ranches. I wondered if L'Amour ever sat in the same booth in his hungry days, hustling up New York editors for overdue payment. I'll bet he had. Now it was my turn. I was young and this was part of the adventure.

But the bastards still didn't send me my check.

I was beginning to understand. In looking for new novelists outside the New York area, what Manor Books was really doing was trolling the boonies for writers who were good enough to be published, but who wouldn't have the clout or the resources to collect the money owed them. Manor would essentially be taking on books for free and walking away with 100% of the profits—Like I said—thieving scuzzballs.

Among my customers at the book exchange was a nice guy with whom I'd become friends. His story was he'd been burned out while being a big city lawyer. At the time, he was on a soul search—holed up in a snowy mountain town in the middle of nowhere, honing his skills as a mime. He was an avid reader. And guess what? He still had his license to practice law in the state of New York.

"How's about this?" I suggested over beer and pizza down at Farquart's. "You get me that grand the sons of bitches owe me and you can waltz in and out of my shop anytime you want and take home as many books as you want for

"His eyes lit up. Some killer instincts do die hard, even in one who'd rather be a mime than a lawyer."

as long as the shop exists." His eyes lit up. Some killer instincts do die hard, even in one who'd rather be a mime than a lawyer.

He said, "Here's what we'll do. Find out if your publisher has done this to anyone else. Then I'll fire off a registered letter to them on my New York stationary. We'll threaten to sue for the thousand and for damages. And if they're doing this to other writers though the mail, we'll threaten to charge them under Federal law with conspiracy to defraud using the US Postal System."

Well, all right.

First thing I did was go down to the local book and magazine store (remember those) that was stocked with Manor titles. I wrote down the names of the authors of those books, and then went about searching for their addresses. My primary resource was the library reference work, Contemporary Authors. I made contact with two writers: Ralph Hayes, an active and not bad pulpist living in Florida (Manor had published his **Check Force** series) and James Holding, the author of a western.

Around this time, I received a letter from another new writer, James Reasoner, who'd sold his first novel to Manor, but was having trouble getting paid and was hearing bad things about them. What did I know? I'd been reading and enjoying James' stories in Mike Shayne, which by then had become a showcase for the emerging talent of my generation.

The following paragraph from my return letter to James (dated 4/4/80) pretty much captures the situation at that point.

All you have heard about Manor is only too true. They currently owe me a grand and the matter is now in the hands of my attorney. They were supposed to pay on publication and that was eight months ago. The lawyer gave them until April 10. But at least they sent me copies of my book! A guy named Jim Holding (not MWA's James Holding, but his grandson) didn't even know his book was out until I spotted it on the stands and wrote him about it. Manor has simply clammed up on him totally to keep from being hassled about on-publication payment. I also exchanged letters with Ralph Hayes. His feeling was Larry Patterson is an okay guy who unfortunately has editorial ambitions outstripping the company's ability to pay promptly. Ralph's advice (and my and Jim Holding's experience bears this out) is to badger Patterson regularly (like every week) via collect phone calls, urging for payment.

The windup: Upon receipt of the mime's registered letter, Manor Books promptly mailed me a check for one thousand dollars.

Manor Books closed shop a few years later. Word gets around.

The mime? Every book he took out of the book exchange, he brought back after he'd read it so I could sell it again. So the whole deal didn't really cost me a penny. I knew good people in Durango in those days.

DAVID 'THE PREACHER' WILSON ON THE THIRD IN THE HARDMAN SERIES WHICH HAVE BEEN REPRINTED BY BRASH BOOKS

THREE THE HARD WAY

Men's Adventure series from the 1970's tend to be hit and miss.

Often, they are a thorough mixture of graphic sex and violence that pushed the boundaries of good taste. However, from 1974-77, Ralph Dennis had twelve books published by Popular Library in The Hard Man series that was hard-boiled and gritty without being erotic or gruesome. The series took its title from an unlicensed private eye, accompanied by his black pal Hump, a former NFL player. The novels are set in Atlanta, Georgia and the reader can feel almost feel the humidity or the "cols", as Dennis describes it.

Of course, the elephant in the novel (rather than the room) is the relationship between Hardman and Hump. Here are two guys who are fully aware that they come from different cultural backgrounds and yet simply deal with it. Spenser does this in his Parker novels with Spenser and Hawk, though at times there is more racial tension between the two. Joe Lansdale does it later in his Hap and Leonard series, complicating it further with Leonard's homosexuality. It's neat to know that as early as the 1970's authors could write about people from different backgrounds with tolerance being demonstrated.

Hardman is a former cop, no longer with the department because of his involvement in a scandal. He does not bother to seek a license and works both sides of the law. In fact, from time to time he acts as a drug mule for the mob. His boundaries are different than what we normally see in our heroes and it adds strength to the characterization. The fact that he is not a cop and does not adhere to police procedure allows him to interrogate people differently, pursue clues differently, and even exact revenge.

"Hardman is a former cop, no longer with the department because of his involvement in a scandal. He does not bother to seek a license and works both sides of the law."

Working both sides of the law, Hardman finds himself in conflict with both police and the mob. In the first two books he develops a relationship with "The Man," a black mob boss. Their relationship becomes very reciprocal, but "The Man" seeks to keep his relationship with Hardman undercover, unwilling to have it known that he cooperates with Hardman.

Hump and Hardman are concerned about the little guy, but they are not adverse to seeking ways to feather their own nests. For example, in the second book of the series they are hunting down a gang of youthful robbers to protect them from the mob hitman that is after them.

Despite helping keep a young man alive for his grandmother they are thinking about getting their hands on at least some of the stolen loot. The author creates a balance between humanitarian and mercenary purposes.

Hardman's Cop friend, Art, talks a good game about police procedure and how Hardman needs to stop holding back information, but all along he knows that Hardman and Hump are not straight arrows. He often bends rules in the name of friendship. In the second book, he almost assuredly is aware that Hump and Hardman are taking some of the loot, but barely acknowledges that fact.

Hump and Hardman alternate back and forth in "good cop-bad cop" when fishing for information. Their occasional disagreements

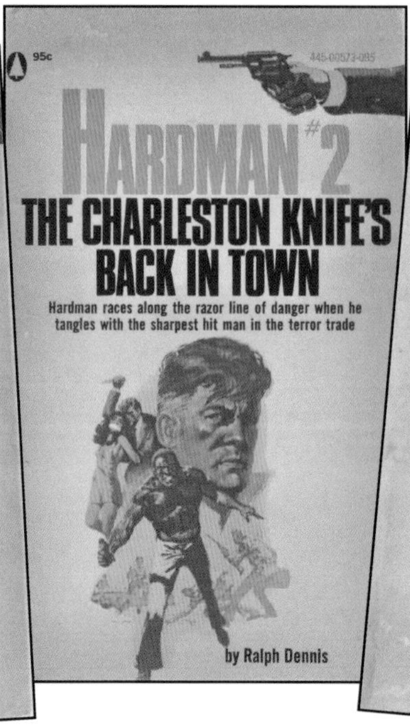

over who should play which role are amusing and reveal their respect for one another. In fact, at times, they switch mid-interrogation as if they can read one another's minds. Their individual roles are usually chosen based on the ethnicity or background of the one they are interrogating.

In **The Golden Girl and All**, the third instalment, Hardman continues crashing through the underworld of 1970's era Atlanta, clashing with cops and crooks alike in his quest for justice. Sadly, in the middle of this conflict is a poor little girl. The primary motivation for Hardman is getting the girl back, but his is also motivated in obtaining justice for an old friend from his policing days.

Hardman is brought in by a lawyer and asked to locate the little girl who is the victim of a parental kidnapping. The mother is the likely suspect and she has a history of drugs and rotten boyfriends. She apparently is a wild vixen in the bedroom, but always attracts the wrong sort of men.

It is important to remember that Hardman has no credentials. A former cop, Hardman simply does favours for people in exchange for cash. He even occasionally smuggles dope for a local drug dealer.

Hardman manages to get a line on the little girl's location almost immediately. Of course, along the way there is a dead body, the brother of a legendary cop now crippled and thus retired. The girl is kidnapped from the mother because she has several pounds of high-grade, uncut, heroin. The poor little girl's situation gives this novel more emotion than the first two novels in the series.

In fact, this novel has much more emotion seeping from the pages than the other novels. The author manages conjure powerful emotion as the possibility of the cop's dead brother being crooked emerges and appears likely. Another of the cops, a tough and brash man, seeks to protect his friend from this knowledge in a display of extreme loyalty. This loyal display gives the reader cause to like the tough cop who is otherwise unlikeable. Amid a cast of unscrupulous and selfish characters this cop was a nice reality touchstone.

The strongest emotional material, however, was in the author's ability to describe the affliction of the injured cop. Dennis works magic as he describes the sound of the crutches, the sound of the breathing, the weariness, and the broken spirit of this man. Everyone around him feels his pain as he walks about. The reader is never permitted to forget that this man was once a legendary servant of justice and now is simply suffering through the remainder of his life.

Hardman and Hump like to drink and they always find a way to have a bottle on hand. They are not drunks, but they always have a way to find a bottle somewhere. Sometimes they use the liquor to ingratiate themselves with underworld types or to obtain information. In one scene, a bottle of peach wine is used to bait an old wino into providing information.

Dennis describes Atlanta lovingly. One area, the Underworld, a run-down area below a set of train tracks. While this is 1970's Atlanta, my curiosity was piqued by the description of this area. At the time of the writing the goal of a group was to bring about a revival of the area and make it an area for viable businesses. Reading this book, I wondered if that goal was later successful.

As usual in this genre, there is plenty of action and violence. There are enough double-crosses to generate tension. And all along the way, the motives of the girl's mother are in question. The reader at times despises her and at others is led to empathize with her, waiting for the conclusion to discover if she is going to act in the child's interest or her own. The conclusion is perhaps the best in the series thus far.

Hardman and his partner, Hump, go to visit the crippled cop to explain his brother's death. There is a moving scene where they all sit down to play a hand of poker as they discuss the details. This ties the novel into a fine conclusion and really humanizes all of the surviving characters. This time around, Hardman's strong external nature is softened by the need of the little girl. This is not a dash for cash, a need for revenge, or a race to survive. The rescue of the little girl becomes the novel's focus and gives it strength. A very well-written thriller.

The **Hardman** series is gritty and suspenseful. This was written in the early days of "men's fiction." One expects it to be violent and sexy, but though there are sexual moments, they are never erotic or graphic.

The main caveat for the reader is to remember that this series was written in the 1970's and some of the attitudes of some characters towards race may prove offensive. However, the friendship between Hump and Hardman more than balances out the racist jerks that pop up from time to time.

"Rainey signed on with the Rhodesian army for the bloodiest campaign in all of Africa!"

...Is the tagline stamped on the first entry on one of my favourite book series', **Soldier of Fortune**. Starring Jim Rainey and his signature Spanish Star .38 handgun, this American gun for hire went on a total of 19 missions, 18 official and 1 unofficial. I will detail what I mean by the latter later in the article.

I first found this series through the wallet-straining reviews on the Paperback Warrior blog, who reviewed the first book in the series, **The Massacre at Umtali**. I was immediately drawn in by that scan of the cover, with the guns blazing and Belmont Tower's signature typeface and styling promising action set in the bloody Rhodesian Bush War. The review was high praise, lauding McCurtin's lean writing prowess and the nonstop pace of the novel. I was sold and soon had a copy in my hands, which promptly got devoured faster than Rainey's Star .38 could chew through another guerilla.

"...I was immediately drawn in by that scan of the cover, with the guns blazing and promising action set in the bloody Rhodesian Bush War."

The series was the brainchild of Belmont Tower author-editor Peter McCurtin. He supplied the first three novels in the series, **The Massacre at Umtali, The Deadliest Game,** and **Spoils of War**. It began in 1976 and ran for two years, before ending in 1978 with **Battle Pay**. Six years later in 1984 the series was revived for another 9 volumes, starting with **Yellow Rain** and, due to declining sales, ended a year later with **Blood Island**. In between both runs Leisure books published a mercenary action novel titled **The Killing Ground** by John Hardesty in 1978. Hardesty was most likely a pen name for Ralph Hayes, who wrote all the subsequent volumes in the first run after McCurtin's three entries. Enticed by the cover, which features a cigar chomping soldier wielding a rocket launcher and a plot set in Northern Ireland during The Troubles, I was pleasantly surprised when I cracked it open. The novel reads just like a Soldier of Fortune book, right down to the Star .38 handgun wielded by our hero, now called Joe Briggs. This was clearly a SoF manuscript that was used after the series was scrapped for the first time around in February of '78, just with a name change. For the curious, the book was excellent, with some great car chases down tight Irish streets and a finale chillingly similar to the IRA mortar attacks 13 years later.

Several authors worked on the series aside from McCurtin, notably Ralph Hayes, who as mentioned penned the rest of the first run and the final volume in the second. He was a good replacement, matching McCurtin's style well,

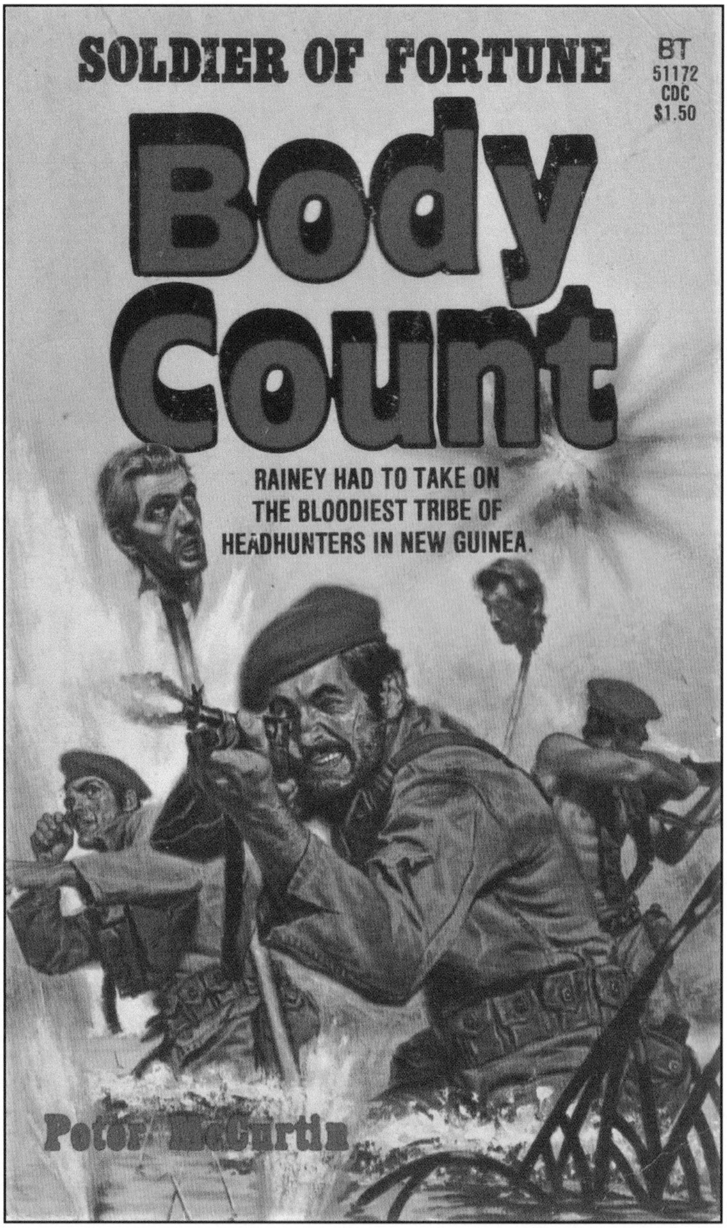

"...One of the most enduring aspects of these books was the cover art. From the cover of that first book that propelled me to purchase that fated first volume, we have some great action-packed art pieces from Mel Crair in the first run of the series."

if a bit more detailed in his prose. I didn't even realize the authorship had changed until the fifth book or so. There is less certainty behind most of the authors in the second run during the 80s, as several have not been copyrighted. I haven't read any and can't comment on them, except to note that **Somali Smashout** was copyrighted to Paul Hofrichter and diverges from the usual style with a third person narrative.

The stories themselves are straightforward guns-blazing yarns typical of Men's Adventure fare. They wouldn't be in this volume if they weren't! They are set in a variety of exotic locales from the rural African wilderness or the jungles of New Guinea to the more metropolitan British Hong Kong and Derry, Northern Ireland. Jim Rainey is often hired to lead an irregular force against some stability threatening guerillas, although this isn't always the case, such as in a race to secure valuable military cargo in Kenya in **Ambush at Derati Wells** or on a mixed revenge-espionage adventure in **Operation Hong Kong**. They are all (save the previously noted exception) written in the first-person perspective, which gives them a more personable feel and lets the reader connect well with Rainey - as well as letting the brutal action explode right in their face! The pace set by McCurtin is a brisk one.

As an author he wasn't known for a lot of laborious set-up to his plots. A 'meat and potatoes' author if there ever was one, with straightforward plots and action every chapter to keep things from getting boring. From ambushes to fistfights to tense arguments with his subordinates that have a tendency of boiling over, they're never boring in the red-blooded violence department. Lean plots and no filler were the order of the day, with little in the way of extraneous details or characterization in novels by either the author-editor or Hayes. Characters are painted in broad strokes, with little unnecessary aspects (if any), but don't ever feel like caricatures or cardboard cutouts. It's all well done and doesn't ever feel forced or too over the top/cartoony.

One of the most enduring aspects of these books was the cover art. From the cover of that first book that propelled me to purchase that fated first volume, we have some great action-packed art pieces from Mel Crair in the first run of the series. I'm not sure of the relationship between Belmont-Tower and Tower Books at this point or through the 70s and 80s, but two visually separate lines appeared: One from Tower books, numbered and featuring a gun-wielding Rainey standing against a plain white background, and another from Belmont-Tower with Rainey and cohorts in action against a solid colored background. My personal preference is for the latter.

In the UK, the series was published first by New English Library and later by Ace/Stoneshire books, who used the Tower books' art for a few of their editions. NEL put out several volumes with new art by Tony Masero and later reprinted them with artwork from David McAllister and the series title "**Jim Rainey: Death Dealer**." The multiple printings suggested their popularity. I don't have a complete listing of what volumes made it across the pond; at least numbers 2-6 were published in the UK by NEL, including one thick 3 volume entry, and 7-9 by Ace/Stoneshire. The rebooted entries weren't so fortunate. Eschewing painted covers, likely for costs, Leisure Books featured photo covers starring a muscular and mustachioed man in action poses. The moustache alone makes the covers so laughably bad and I don't think that even in the 80s they would have helped sell copies. In Australia, Horowitz republished **Spoils of War**, **Battle Pay, and The Killing Ground**. Surprisingly, **Operation Hong Kong** received a Braille edition from the Queensland Braille Writing Association, although I have no other info on this besides the copyright record. The series was exported outside of the Anglo-

"...NEL put out several volumes with new art by Tony Masero and later reprinted them with artwork from David McAllister."

Soldier of Fortune #3: Spoils of War
Peter McCurtin
1976

Let me begin this review with a strong personal opinion of mine: This book is my favourite **Soldier of Fortune** book to date. As far as I'm concerned, it's the perfect book. I might even say it's one of my favourite Men's Adventure novels of all time. If my review comes across as too glowing, that's why.

The book opens with Jim Rainey, mercenary extraordinaire, being hunted by professional assassin Joe Maltese in Israel. McCurtin gives us the tension of the hunt in the first chapter and the stress of a frantic hand-to-hand fight for his life in the second, leading to an explosive finish that leaves Rainey alive and the world-renowned hitman very much dead. This gives him a reputation that will help him secure his next contract in Lebanon and will end up following him in the next book or two, a rare recurring plot point in a series consisting of self-contained adventures.

In Lebanon, Rainey is tasked with stopping the Sons of Islam, a violent Druze Islamist group opposing the current government, led by Ibrahim Sharif. Despite not giving a damn about religious politics, he is appointed the head of the Christian militant group the New Disciples to crush this threat. This plot might seem kind of touchy in today's post-9/11 world, but I suppose American readers in 1976 didn't give much of a damn about foreign religious politics either. Back then, it was all framed in the lens that audiences at the time would understand it: East vs West, with the Muslims being backed by Moscow and the Christians by the West.

McCurtin keeps the action up in practically every chapter, with guerrilla ambushes along the tense journey out to the New Disciples camp and contending with the two rival lieutenants he was assigned, Halfin and Brussard. What follows is a well-trod (but well-done) plot line: Rainey must get the demoralized group in fighting shape, as well as sorting out the differences between his Lieutenants. The violence only ratchets up after establishing their base, where both sides wage quick and devastating strikes on one another. Nothing is held back, and the body count is high. The reader hardly gets a moment to breathe before there are shouts for "Take cover!" and "Return fire!"

This is all helped by the signature first-person narration that became a staple to the series and lent a personal touch, helping to connect the reader with the hero and sucking them into the story. I could hardly set the book down lest I get blind-sided by a surprise mortar attack or a **Rat Patrol**-esque hit-and-run. It all culminates in the last third of the novel with a final blistering confrontation filled with close calls, jeep run-and-guns, and an enemy that only just keeps managing to get away.

There is plenty of his signature hand-to-hand fighting all through this novel, from an encounter with a sword-wielding Muslim to a leadership-establishing bare-knuckle brawl with Brussard, and this is before the cigarette ad! The gunplay is excellent and of the usual brutality, though not overly-gory. As previously mentioned, nothing stops for more than a minute or two, with readers being treated to a new life-or-death encounter every chapter. McCurtin is a veteran in the field and this pace doesn't get stale under him.

With the two books that he wrote previously, **The Massacre at Umtali** and **The Deadliest Game,** this novel makes for a nice unofficial trilogy of top-tier mercenary fiction. Overall, this entry and the ones previous have all of the things I love about the **Soldier of Fortune** books: a suitably exotic locale, a nonstop pace, military-esque guerrilla warfare, bone-crunching hand-to-hand combat, and a good cast of colourful supporting characters. A must read for fans of the series and fans of Men's Adventure fiction in general.

Sean Nodland

sphere; In the Netherlands, **The Massacre at Umtali** and **Ambush at Derati Wells** were translated into Dutch and republished in the late 70s under the Bazooka line of either paperback or magazine reprints. Considering both stories' South African/Boer setting I'm sure these were attractive to the former colonial overlords. In the early 90s a handful of titles were translated into Polish and published by Aramis under the reprint line "Czarna Pantera" (Black Panther in English). The line translated and published reprints of several American Men's Adventure war novels after the fall of the Soviet Union. I also can't speak to the quality of the translations or how well they were received. The titles that made the jump were, in order of Polish publication, **Spoils of War**, **Battle Pay**, **Green Hell**, **The Deadliest Game**, and **The Massacre at Umtali**.

I have always liked the concept of mercenaries in fiction; they give the best plausible deniability for being an antihero or morally ambiguous protagonist: they're just doing it for a paycheck. No matter what ethically dubious endeavour needs undertaking you can use a Merc to be your protagonist and get away (quite literally) with murder. The trope seems to have only really lived on in a large part in the science fiction genre, and even then, the "morally ambiguous" bit isn't really emphasized. I also think that these books have, in a way, gotten better with age; the period of cold war decolonisation, the death of the last vestiges of imperialism, and proxy wars with the Soviets was over before I was born. Conflicts like the Rhodesian Bush War, The Troubles, and various Communist insurgencies are relics of a previous era of conflicts whose true nature seem far more amoral (or even immoral) with hindsight and differing values today than they might have been in their time. These settings combined with the unique first-person narrative style that was coupled with McCurtin's sparse prose, made for gripping tales that really ought to be appreciated beyond this "disposable fiction." His unique writing style was a thing all his own, and we're lucky to have it live on in these books today.

Do yourself a favour: strap on your combat boots, pick up a copy of one of these books, and let Rainey tell you about another of his rugged, death-defying exploits over cigars and cold drinks. Trust me - you won't be disappointed!

I would like to thank Lynn Munroe for the background info on the origins and demise of the series, his website is an invaluable one for biographical research on Peter McCurtin. I would also like to thank Justin for his informational input on the various artists for the series covers. And I would like to thank the Paperback Warrior blog for introducing me to this and many other great paperback books.

BOB DEIS AND BILL CUNNINGHAM UNLEASH THEIR NEW FANZINE, STORY AND ART ANTHOLOGY COMBO - THE MEN'S ADVENTURE QUARTERLY

ENTER THE MAQ

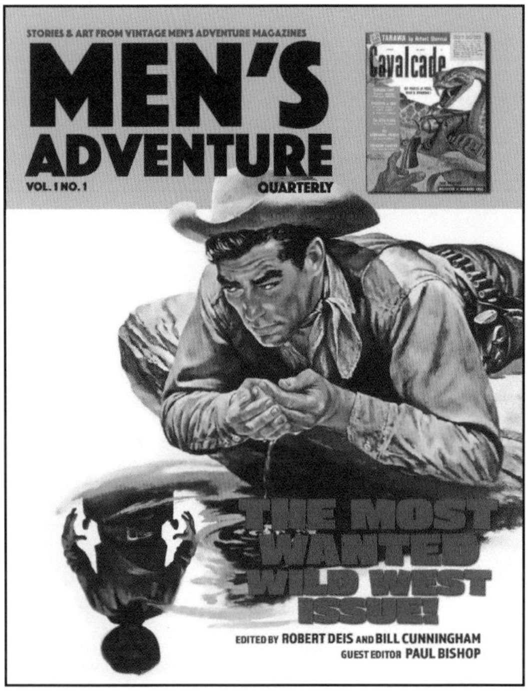

Justin - Bob and Bill, please tell the readers about your goals and ambitions for your exciting new publication.

BOB: The **Men's Adventure Quarterly** is part of my devious overall plan as a writer, editor and publisher to increase awareness and appreciation of vintage men's adventure magazines published in the '50s, '60s, and '70s. The MAM genre hasn't been given the level of attention in terms of books, fanzines or websites that's been given to the pulp magazines MAMs are partly descended from, or to mid-20th century paperbacks, which have many connections to MAMs. All three of those genres have overlaps in the artists, writers and publishers involved, and in the types of stories they feature. But when I first started collecting them a couple of decades ago, I discovered that there weren't many books about them, or anthologies that collected stories and artwork from them, like there are for the pulps. And, there weren't any websites or fanzines dedicated to them. So, about 10 years ago, after I had amassed a collection of over 6,000 MAM issues and had learned quite a bit about them, I created a blog focused on MAMs, MensPulpMags.com. Then I started a Facebook group, the Men's Adventure Magazines & Books Group.

Through those, I started making connections with some of the living writers, artists, editors and models who worked for MAMs and with other people who appreciated MAM stories and artwork. That led me to want to fill the void in books that reprinted MAM stories and artwork and discussed their history and context. One of the people I connected with was Wyatt Doyle, founder of the New Texture imprint. In 2013, Wyatt and I launched a line of books featuring MAM stories and artwork. We now have twelve books in the series and plan to keep publishing several more each year. The Quarterly is partly inspired by your vintage paperback fanzines, Justin. I really love the way they showcase and discuss the history of the various paperback subgenres. They inspired me to start thinking about doing a MAM fanzine. But as I thought about it, I realized most people would not be able to buy copies of the MAM issues. You can generally find copies of vintage paperbacks you're interested in or eBook reprints, at reasonable costs. But there aren't lots of copies of most MAM issues that are easily available and inexpensive. So, while most people may have read or could read paperbacks you discuss in your fanzines, that wouldn't be the case with MAMs. I had admired some of the layout work of Bill Cunningham and asked him what he

"My ideal ambition is for the MAQ to help make a lot of people around the world more aware of and interested in the Men's Adventure Magazine (MAM) genre..."

thought about helping me create a sort of hybrid between a fanzine and the books I do with Wyatt Doyle and he loved the idea. He created some concept layouts that knocked my socks off and had some great ideas for what we'd feature in an issue. Within a couple of months of hatching the idea and hashing out the approach, we had the first issue ready to go. My ideal ambition is for the **MAQ** to help make a lot of people around the world more aware of and interested in the MAM genre.

BILL: For me, it was the chance to capture the excitement of men's adventure magazines for both the classic readers, and new fans of the form. It was also a challenge that I threw at myself to create a look for this magazine that gives it the energy that the men's adventure magazines embody. I didn't want to just recreate the old stuff, but I wanted to push it into new areas that we are all familiar with when it comes to this pulpy material. In that way, I'll be using the men's magazines, action movies, paperbacks, comics, and other material in my attempt to fuse the story with the visual. You know me, It's all pulp.
Ultimately, I want readers to enjoy the magazine and be able to get a glimpse at the men's adventure experience. I like doing this and when someone has something nice to say about something I've written or published or has a really insightful piece of criticism - I'm stoked. It tells me people care, and part of my job is to get them to care.

I really liked the idea of the first issue having a theme, in this case, Westerns. What themes will you be dealing with in future issues?

BOB: In my initial discussions with Bill I raised the idea of having each issue focus on stories and artwork related to a particular subject. Over the years, I have been stashing away lists of MAM stories and artwork by topic and I knew there were scores of topics we could cover. We picked Westerns as the theme of the first issue partly because we'd noticed the recent upsurge of interest in that genre. In addition to your great **Hot Lead** fanzine, we'd noticed an increase in reprints of old Western novels and the publication of many new ones by indie publishers we admire, like Wolfpack Publishing, Airship 27, Bold Venture and Piccadilly Press. We had also become fans of the **Six-Gun Justice** podcast about Western novels, TV shows and movies that became hugely popular soon after it was launched in 2020 by novelist Paul Bishop. Of course, he's has been a major contributor to your **Hot Lead** fanzine. I'm an especially big fan of Paul's and we've become long distance friends. Bill knows Paul, too. So we ran the Quarterly idea up the flagpole with him. He liked it and agreed that Westerns would be a cool and timely theme to start with. I'm honoured that Paul agreed to write a Guest Editorial for our initial issue. Having collected and read a lot of MAM issues, I can tell you that the options for future topics are enormous. MAMs include fictions stories and non-fiction articles on just about everything. Some of the topics that I'm particularly partial to are Cold War spies, Civil War stories, exotic adventure yarns, survival stories, killer creature stories, stories featuring femme fatales and women freedom fighters, detective stories and stories about gangs --- including teenage gangs, girl gangs and motorcycle gangs.

BILL: That was one of the long term questions Bob and I hashed out at the beginning - *what were all the genres that the men's adventure mags covered?* I thought about it and sent Bob a three-page document outlining my thoughts on the genres, the distribution, the marketing - all of it. I came up with 24 different story types [not even scratching the surface really because I didn't account for factual articles in my thinking] that would account for 6 years worth of work. Bob informs me that we could do multiple western issues, multiple crime, multiple war, etc... volumes of MAQ. In the short term, we will be dealing with westerns, espionage, and other genres that are familiar to the men's adventure audience and others.

In the first issue, you explore the influence of the MAMs on the adult western paperback genre, which I found fascinating.

BILL: Visually, there are a lot of the MAMs that used many of the same artists and models for their covers as the paperback industry. It makes sense that the visual elements of the MAMs would "cross over" to the less-frequently published paperbacks. The stories in the MAMs were also rougher - meaning more violent and sexy - than mainstream publications so you had this atmosphere of telling the juiciest stories illustrated with the juiciest artwork. I think the publishers saw what was working in the MAMs and moved in that direction. Bob can speak to the crossover of the writers, but I can think of one right now - who is published in this first issue - that was hugely influential and successful in the adult western genre.

BOB: I actually learned about the adult Western paperback genre from your fanzines and people who hang out in the Men's Adventure Paperbacks of the 20th Century Facebook group, which include a number of writers who have actually written adult Westerns under their own names or pseudonyms, like Paul Bishop and James Reasoner. That led me to start reading some of the Piccadilly Westerns and some of the long-running American adult Western series, like **Longarm**. In the realm of paperbacks, the adult Western genre arose in the '70s. But I knew from reading Western stories in MAMs published in the '50s and '60s that they often had more sex and more graphic violence than the Western paperbacks that were published in those decades, before the adult Western genre was launched. I also realized that some of the notable writers of adult Westerns had previously written Western stories for MAMs --- most notably Lou Cameron, who created the **Longarm**, **Renegade** and **Stringer** adult Western series. The descriptions of sex in adult Westerns is more graphic than what MAMs could get away with in the '50s and '60s, but they pushed the envelope on that front in their descriptions of bloody violence. Our initial issue of the Quarterly includes some examples of precursors to the adult

Shoot-Out at Mad Sadie's Place

It was a red-silk saloon with a whale-sized madame and six killers from Texas in a town that didn't care—the perfect setting for the vengeance of Luken's last fight.

by DONALD HONIG

THE LONE rider came through a stand of cottonwood into the bright sunshine on the bluff and gently reined in his horse. He brought his fist up to his mouth and absently chewed a knuckle as he stared down the bluff at Indian Skull, a gold-strike town that was a nondescript collection of frame buildings standing in the bottom of a bowl created by the walls of low-lying hills.

"Indian Skull," Pod Luken said aloud, sarcastically. His eyes continued to rove over the town. Two rows of buildings were divided by the main street, there were several side streets and a few outlying houses. He saw the usual collection of saloons and dance halls and the few necessary stores, a blacksmith's and a stable.

So this was the precious, frightened little town, he thought bitterly. It looked no different (*Continued on page 76*)

Luken dove at the familiar click of the Winchester Repeater, and, as the bullet slapped by him, began fanning his gun at the figures against the fire.

Art by Tom Ruback

32

33

Western paperbacks, including one written by Lou Cameron and one by Dean Ballenger, who wrote some classic ultra-violent novels, like the **Gannon** trilogy.

If you want some more evidence that Western stories in MAMs paved the way for the ultra-violent adult Western novels, check out the story "Bloodiest Mass Murderer of the Old West" that we included. It's by a little-known writer named Grayson Peters and was published in the October 1962 issue of **A-OK For Men**, one of many men's adventure periodicals that only lasted for a handful of issues. In the first page of his story alone, a bad guy named Stanton and his gang of thugs stab a man and his two teenage sons in their stomachs, then slit their throats. Next, they rape the man's wife and daughters, ages 13 and 15. Then they shoot the woman and girls and scalp and burn all the bodies to make it look like Indians did it. That's pretty over-the-top for 1962, and it's just the beginning of this dark and bloody tale.

The magazine is visually striking – how do the pair of you collaborate on the visual elements of the magazine.

BILL: Part of my job is to give the editor what he wants, but more importantly give him what he needs. Bob chooses the stories and provides the art that originally went with them, and I make it work for the Amazon printing format. It all starts with the original artwork and I come up with new ways to use it so it doesn't seem "staid" or worse yet, "boring."

So, I redesign the artwork, remove and replace text, add elements, etc... My job is to make it look great and give the reader his money's worth when he looks at the magazine. I want him (or her!) to be pleased and surprised and turning pages. Bob looks at it all and gives his notes, on things he wants to see for clarity's sake. Overall I think he's been pleased with what I add to the process, and I'm pleased with the material Bob provides me. As I layout his story introductions I am always learning something new that helps me with the next story.

BOB: Well, of course, the original credit for how striking the visuals are start with the artists who worked for the MAM genre. The cover paintings and interior illustrations in MAMs were done by many of the top illustration artists of the era, most of whom also did paperback covers. Artists like Mort Kunstler, James Bama, Gil Cohen, Frank McCarthy, Thomas Beecham, Ernest "Darcy" Chiriaka, Charles Copeland, Norm Eastman, Robert Maguire, James Meese, Bruce Minney, Barye Phillips, Samson Pollen, Al Rossi, John Schoenherr, Robert Schulz, Robert Stanley, Ed Valigursky --- the list goes on and on. It's mind-boggling mow much great artwork we have to choose from for the Quarterly. And, the way Bill showcases that artwork and reuses pieces of it is extremely creative. He has a fresh way of designing layouts with vintage elements that I really love. I can't wait to see what he does with the layout of our second issues, which will feature spy stories and artwork.

Thanks for talking to me guys - I look forward to seeing the mag in print. I think it will be a huge success!

BLAZING COMBAT

SEAN NODLAND PARACHUTES IN WITH TWO QUICK-FIRE REVIEWS

Punishment Battalion 333 #1
Baptism of Blood
Charles Whiting writing as K N Kostov
1980

In a desperate bid to bolster Soviet morale in defence of Moscow, infamous NKVD Chief Beria creates a battalion of political and criminal prisoners from his gulags. Punishment Battalion 333, a band of "traitors, reactionaries, pimps, whoremasters, black marketeers, murderers and perverts - the worse the labour camps had to offer", is led by the ruthless Colonel Katukov and aided by the (former) Marshal Boldin, a purged marshal of the Soviet Union looking for redemption, who must fight hard to keep the capitol of the USSR from falling into Nazi hands.

Another one of Whiting's military tales, I have to say going in I had forgotten how distinct his writing style is. While I like it, for me personally I can only take it in small doses. While overall good, I had a hard time finishing the novel because I had recently read another of his. If you're a fan of his work you'll find the same stuff to love from a (somewhat) fresh point of view: possibly authentic Soviet military slang, translator/editor footnotes, dire situations for cynical characters, and the ever popular devastating artillery barrage that kills plenty of faceless friendlies and few principle characters. For the uninitiated, this is not a bad entry into his work, but it is nothing stellar. If you would like to read a solid harrowing military tale and for whatever reason do not want to dive into his body of Axis-oriented material, this should do the trick. Perhaps someone else will appreciate it more than me, as I am only giving it 3 gulag rats out of 5.

The Sergeant #2: Hell Harbor
Gordon Davis (Leonard Levinson)
1980

Hell Harbor is the second novel in the 9 book saga of Clarence J. Mahoney, Sergeant of the US Army Rangers. This series, as well as the later **Rat Bastards** series, both penned by genre veteran Leonard Levinson, is one of the most entertaining WW2 series I've read.

After recuperating in a London hospital following his escapade behind the lines in the first book, Sergeant Mahoney is sent back to the front to assist in the assault on the coastal town of Cherbourg. He is sent ahead of the main assault to reconnoiter a Nazi fortress in the town and finds out that they plan to irreparibly bomb the harbor to massively slow the Allied offensive. Mahoney and a squad of

"...The Rat Bastards rolls along like a blitzing tank."

Rangers and Resistance must race against the clock to figure out how to stop this plot.

Len Levinson is known for his good plotting and pacing, his straight action novels like this series and **The Rat Bastards** rolls along like a blitzing tank. The action, while notably less than in the first volume, has a punchy swing to it that he uses to great effect. This is highlighted best in the climactic finale of the book, where The Sergeant and his team get caught up in a claustrophobic infiltration and subsequent gunfight.

However, I believe the hallmarks of the author are his characters and his humor. Sergeant Mahoney is a wonderfully realized protagonist, a self-interested asshole with a begrudgingly honourable streak. His friendship with Corporal Cranepool feels very real, like all of the other relationships Levinson illustrates through his books. The humorous situations that Mahoney finds himself in, like his attempted early hospital discharge to go boozing and whoring on the streets of London, or his attempt to acquire donuts when he returns to the front, left me with quizzical looks from my wife as to why I was laughing so much.

I am a big fan of Len Levinson's work and I believe this series is one of his best. I've not read enough entries in the series to call it the best, I still believe it deserves to be read by any action fan, combat aficionado or no.

4.5 grenades

Printed in Great Britain
by Amazon

54685194R00035